New Employee Orientation TRAINING

D1220604

Includes CD-ROM with Ready-to-Use Microsoft PowerPoint® Presentations

Exercises, Handouts, Assessments, and Tools to Help You:

✔ Rapidly Build a Customized New Employee Orientation Program

✔ Create Both Organization-Wide and Department-Level Training

✔ Become a More Effective and Efficient Facilitator

✔ Ensure Training Is on Target and Gets Results

ASTD
Linking People,
Learning & Performance

Karen Lawson

Published by the American Society for Training & Development (ASTD).

Ordering Information: Books published by ASTD can be ordered by calling 800.628.2783 or 703.683.8100, or via the Website at www.astd.org.

Library of Congress Catalog Card Number: 2002105494

ISBN: 1-56286-318-5

The ASTD Trainer's WorkShop Series is designed to be a practical, hands-on road map to help you quickly develop training in key business areas. Each book in the series offers all the exercises, handouts, assessments, structured experiences, and ready-to-use presentations needed to develop effective training sessions. In addition to easy-to-use icons, each book in the series includes a companion CD-ROM with PowerPoint presentations and electronic copies of all supporting material featured in the book.

Other books in the Trainer's WorkShop Series:

- *New Supervisor Training*
  John E. Jones and Chris W. Chen

- *Customer Service Training*
  Maxine Kamin

- *Leading Change Training*
  Jeffrey Russell and Linda Russell

- *Coaching Training*
  Chris W. Chen

- *Leadership Training*
  Lou Russell

C o n t e n t s

◆

Every day in organizations around the world, people start new jobs, eager, excited, and anxious but ready to do their best. Within the first few months or even weeks, many of those new employees become discouraged and disillusioned, often as a direct result of the way in which they were introduced to the organization. In far too many cases, new employees are thrown into their new environment and are expected to sink or swim.

Because of my experiences as an employee in corporate America and later as an external consultant and training professional, I recognized the need for a process to help the new employee adapt and assimilate more quickly and successfully into his or her new work environment. In my interviews with employees in several different types of organizations and industries, I heard story after story of the unpleasant experiences of new hires during their first days, weeks, and months on the job. I also talked with people responsible for new employee orientation in their organizations to get an idea of what works and what doesn't. Based on those interviews, a literature search, and my experience in cooperative learning and interactive training techniques, I decided to offer a more interactive and process-driven approach to new employee orientation programs. My goal was to provide a workbook that can be used to create an effective new employee orientation program in any organization, regardless of its size. The designs and activities are easily adapted to any situation. They can be used as stand-alone programs or to enhance an existing program. The step-by-step instructions make it easy for anyone to follow.

You will notice that I have used very few slides in the program modules. Because my goal is to make new employee orientation programs highly interactive and participant-centered, I have kept a straight presentation approach to a minimum. Consistent with adult learning principles, the participants will learn by *doing,* not by being told.

I would not have been able to write this workbook without the help of others. First, I extend my gratitude to my clients and the many participants in my training programs who openly shared their experiences, insights, and suggestions with me. I am also grateful to Mark Morrow, acquisitions editor for the

American Society for Training & Development, for his support, encouragement, and patience.

As with other book projects, this was a labor of love, and I hope that those who use this workbook and those who benefit from its application will approach their everyday workplace experiences with renewed enthusiasm and a heightened sense of purpose.

Karen Lawson
June 2002

Introduction: How to Use This Book Effectively

What's in This Chapter?

◆ Discussion of the importance of new employee orientation

◆ Description of the target audience

◆ Explanation of how to use this book

Employees are an organization's most valuable resource, but the way most organizations "welcome" a new employee creates the opposite impression. Organizations often approach orientation as an afterthought. Others spend thousands of dollars and a great deal of time and effort on slick PowerPoint presentations, multiple guest speakers, and voluminous employee handbooks, all of which leave the new employee dazed, anxious, and overwhelmed. Why do they do that?

For starters, the typical new employee orientation program is boring. Like many other traditional training programs, it is presenter-centered and lecture-driven, with little or no opportunity for participant interaction. That approach is characterized by too many facts, figures, and faces packed into a few hours. And when the new employee finally gets to the actual work site, it's obvious no one is prepared for his or her arrival.

The orientation program really is the employee's first exposure to the organization; therefore, it should be an enjoyable and memorable experience. Because it sets the tone, this program needs to be a priority item. A thoughtfully planned and delivered program helps the employee's transition, prompts him or her to feel good about the organization, and ignites excitement and enthusiasm. The focus should be on helping to integrate the new employee into the organization and to begin building relationships.

Organizations that skimp on orientation programs not only shortchange the employee; they also miss the perfect opportunity to communicate and help the employee embrace and internalize the organization's philosophy, values, norms, and culture. Employees need to understand how they fit into the big picture—that what they do is important and makes a difference. The orientation program can help the new employee become more comfortable, confident, and competent.

An effective new employee orientation program takes time and effort but is well worth the investment. Studies show that a well-planned, comprehensive orientation program greatly benefits both the organization and the employees. Researchers at Ohio State University "found that new employees who completed a three-hour orientation program showed a higher level of commitment than did those who skipped the program" (Grabmeier, March 28, 2000). Furthermore, the "increased commitment resulted from the fact that those who attended had a better understanding of the organization's goals and values and knew more about its history than those who didn't go" (Grabmeier, March 28, 2000). Increased commitment leads to increased employee retention.

First and foremost, a new employee orientation must be approached as a process, not an event. Employees should receive information on a need-to-know basis (so as not to overwhelm) to help them move into and adapt to their new environment.

Understanding How and Why People Learn

Adult learning theory serves as the basis for any effective training program, and a new employee orientation program should be no exception. The following assumptions underlie the andragogical model of learning, which Malcolm Knowles now calls a model of human learning (Knowles, 1990).

◆ **Adults need self-direction.** Adult learners want to take responsibility for their own lives, including the planning, implementing, and evaluating of their learning activities. From the beginning, the trainer needs to establish the training process as a collaborative effort. Throughout the process, the trainer and participant should be partners engaged in ongoing, two-way communication. This approach also provides the model and sets the expectation for two-way communication between the supervisor and the employee.

◆ **Adults' past experiences are integral.** According to Knowles, each of us brings to a learning situation a wealth of experiences that provide a base for new learning and a resource to share with others. Whether good or bad, these experiences certainly affect the way in which an employee approaches a new learning situation. Because people base their learning on past experiences, the new information must be assimilated. The smart trainer will find out what the participants already know and will build on that experience, with activities and structured experiences, rather than treating participants as if they know nothing and must be *taught* like small children.

◆ **Adults must recognize a need to learn.** Adults are ready to learn when they perceive a need to know or do something in order to perform more effectively in some aspect of their lives. They want the learning experience to be practical and realistic, problem-centered rather than subject-centered. The effective trainer will provide new employees with information they *need* to know and not overwhelm them with facts and figures that have no relevance to their jobs. Trainers also will help new employees see how they fit into the larger picture.

◆ **Adults are motivated by real-world application.** Adults want the skills and knowledge to help them solve problems or complete tasks. People are moved to learn when they see relevance to their real-life situations and quickly are able to apply what they have learned. Therefore, learning activities must be clearly relevant to their immediate needs. New employees want to know specific information about the organization that will help them assimilate more quickly.

◆ **Adults need a variety of training methods.** New employees represent a variety of learning styles, so the effective new employee orientation program will incorporate a variety of methods to engage each participant.

Target Audience

Trainers and human resources professionals can use this resource to design and conduct an organization-level orientation program consistent with the organization's culture and philosophy. They also can use it to help train line managers and supervisors in orienting their new employees. Line managers and supervisors may use it themselves to create a more effective and meaningful orientation experience for their new employees. Specifically, this workbook will help readers to

- identify the universal concerns of new employees

- develop pleasant, memorable, and productive new employee orientation programs at both organization and department levels.

What This Workbook Includes

The aim of this workbook is to equip those who are charged with new employee orientation responsibilities with the tools and techniques to design and conduct a highly interactive program that is targeted at the needs of today's employees and those of the organization. The following tools and techniques will help you create a highly interactive program:

- **Methods and effective practices** for communicating critical information about the organization

- **Training modules** that may be used as is or can be modified to meet specific needs

- **Tips and tricks** for effective facilitation of the new employee orientation program

- **Evaluation methods and effective practices** for new employee orientation programs, including tools for facilitator assessment and approaches that encourage continuous improvement

- **Learning activities** applicable to a variety of situations.

Using This Workbook Most Effectively

This workbook presents a practical how-to approach to developing a comprehensive new employee orientation program. It addresses what should be included in an organization-wide program conducted by human resources personnel and in programs that are department specific and conducted by line managers or supervisors.

The book contains activities designed to make the orientation programs interactive and personally engaging for the new employee. It also includes reproducible forms, such as checklists, letters, and evaluation forms, that supervisors, in particular, can use to help make enjoyable and rewarding the first few days and weeks of an employee's new job.

You can use this book to develop your own orientation program. Here are your options:

- ◆ Use the two-day and one-day programs as written (chapter 7)

- ◆ Modify the designs for departmental orientation (chapter 8) or for employees at a distance (chapter 9)

- ◆ Choose specific learning activities (chapter 10) to create your own program

- ◆ Combine some of the learning activities in chapter 10 with your own activities.

Each self-contained session includes detailed instructions for the facilitator as well as recommended timeframes. Within those session designs, you have some flexibility to choose among two or three learning activities by which to communicate your content. Many of the learning activities also include variations of the activity's design and different options for facilitating that activity.

Before selecting your option, use the following approach to gain the most value from this workbook:

1. **Study the book.** Study the entire list of contents of this workbook to get an overview of the resources it contains.

2. **Review the CD.** Review the contents of the accompanying compact disc to see how they relate to the material in the printed book. Open the printable files and the PowerPoint presentation so that you can determine how those materials will enrich your program and which handouts you may want to print and copy. This step should include a careful reading of the appendix, "Using the Compact Disc," at the back of the workbook or *How to Use This CD.txt* on the accompanying CD.

3. **Review chapter 2.** Study and apply the strategies outlined in chapter 2, "Identifying the Orientation Needs of New Employees."

4. **Review chapter 3.** When you have absorbed the information about what a new employee needs, go to chapter 3, "Designing an Interactive Program." Design your session to meet the specific needs of your organization and those who will be attending the new

employee orientation program. Chapter 7 presents a detailed design for both a two-day program and a one-day program. Another option is to choose specific learning activities provided in chapter 10 to create your own program or to combine with or supplement your own activities.

5. **Review chapter 4.** Prepare to implement your training by studying the approaches in chapter 4, "Preparing for a New Employee Orientation Program." Pay particular attention to the recommended time lines.

6. **Review chapter 5.** Become familiar with various facilitation and classroom techniques that will help you deliver dynamic and successful programs.

7. **Review chapter 6.** Plan to evaluate your new employee orientation sessions. Chapter 6, "Evaluating Your New Employee Orientation Program," explains why this is important and provides steps to follow to assess the outcomes of using an interactive approach to new employee orientation. Decide how you want to go about evaluating the program and what methods you wish to use.

8. **Design your training.** Chapters 7 through 9 offer step-by-step instructions for creating orientation programs of varying lengths and for audiences of various sizes and at distant locations. The specific materials found in chapters 10 and 11 (and on the accompanying CD) provide you with appropriate content, structured experiences, and helpful tools.

Icons

For easy reference, icons are included in the outside margins of this workbook so you can identify elements of a chapter or program and easily locate particular tools and handouts. Here are the icons and what they indicate:

CD: Indicates materials included on the CD accompanying this workbook.

Clock: Indicates suggested timeframes for an activity.

Discussion Questions: Points out questions you can use to explore significant facets of the training and debrief participants after the learning activities.

Handout: Indicates handouts you can print or copy and then use in ways that enhance the training experience.

Key Point: Alerts you to key points that should be emphasized in relation to a particular topic.

Learning Activities: Identifies learning activities included in chapter 10.

PowerPoint Item: Indicates PowerPoint slides that can be used jointly or individually. They are on the CD included with your workbook, and small copies of the slides are included in chapter 7. Instructions for using Power-Point slides and the CD are included in the appendix and on the CD.

Tool: Identifies an item that offers useful information for facilitators.

What to Do Next: Indicates recommendations for actions to take after completing a particular section of the text.

What to Do Next

- ◆ Begin meeting with key people in your organization to get support for a comprehensive, structured approach to new employee orientation.

- ◆ Read chapter 2, "Identifying the Orientation Needs of New Employees."

◆ ◆ ◆

The first step in developing an effective new employee orientation program includes identifying the orientation needs of your new employees. The next chapter provides useful insight into the unique traits and characteristics of employees—insights that will enable you to define their needs.

Identifying the Orientation Needs of New Employees

What's in This Chapter?

- Explanations of various learning styles and perceptual modalities to incorporate in orientations
- Discussion of organizational diversity issues that programs must address

Think about your own experiences as a new employee. Did you attend a formal orientation program? If so, how effective was the experience? To what degree did the orientation experience (or lack of it) contribute to your success (or failure)? Keep in mind that a negative experience during the first few days or weeks of employment can have disastrous results. The new employee may quit or, if the employee decides to stay, he or she probably will be demotivated and will work only to collect a paycheck.

In addition to understanding the principles underlying the theory of adult learning discussed in chapter 1, it's important to consider other needs of your new employees before you design your program.

As a trainer, you have a responsibility to create a classroom environment in which all participants feel free to express and be themselves. You can begin to create this environment when you design a program, taking into consideration all types of differences, including learning style differences. Not only should you respect the individual differences of those in your sessions; you must make sure you incorporate into your program design a variety of methods and materials that will accommodate those differences.

Material in this chapter was adapted from The Trainer's Handbook *by Karen Lawson (San Francisco: Jossey-Bass/Pfeiffer, 1998).*

The challenge of meeting the individual needs of participants often may seem overwhelming. Armed with an understanding of today's learners and equipped with a kit of tips, techniques, and tools, you will be able to create an environment that both respects and celebrates differences and sets the tone for what the new employee can expect as a team member.

Learning Styles and Perceptual Modalities

Adults learn through a variety of means. One person may learn better by listening; another person may be visual and prefer to read instructions; someone else may need a demonstration.

No one learning mode is right or even better than another. The point is that each person learns differently, and you will have a variety of learning styles represented in your training attendees. Effective trainers, therefore, must design their programs to accommodate such style differences.

An effective trainer must understand the different perceptual modalities; that is, the ways in which people take in and process information. According to W.B. James and M.W. Galbraith (1985), a learner may prefer one of the following six perceptual modalities:

1. **Visual:** Videos, slides, graphs, photos, demonstrations—methods and media that create opportunities for the participant to experience learning through the eyes

2. **Print:** Texts, paper-and-pencil exercises—activities that enable the participant to absorb the written word

3. **Aural:** Lectures, audiotapes—methods that allow the participant simply to listen and take in information through the ears

4. **Interactive:** Group discussions, question-and-answer sessions—opportunities to talk and exchange ideas, opinions, and reactions with fellow participants

5. **Tactile:** Hands-on activities, model building—activities that require the participant to handle objects or put things together

6. **Kinesthetic:** Role plays, physical games—activities that involve the use of psychomotor skills and movement from one place to another.

Research indicates that more adults learn visually than by any other perceptual style. A good training design, however, will incorporate all six modalities to ensure that every trainee's needs are being addressed. You need to vary activities to create multisensory learning that increases the likelihood of appealing to each participant's style and helps reinforce the knowledge or skills acquired through the preferred modality.

Another important consideration is that people generally *learn by doing*, not by being told how to do something. For example, a person learns more quickly how to get to a new location by driving the car rather than merely observing as a passenger. The more opportunities one has to try out or apply new skills, the more likely he or she is to learn those skills.

Telling is not teaching or training. How many times have you said to yourself, "I've told him and told him how to do it, but he still gets it wrong"? Just because you tell someone how to do something doesn't mean he or she understands it or has developed the skill to do the task.

The Changing Organizational Environment

The organizational landscape has changed dramatically and will continue to change in the future. A diverse workforce has altered not only the way companies do business but also the way they train their workers. In addition to the various modalities we just explored, differences such as age, gender, race, ethnicity, lifestyle, religion, language, disabilities, and literacy affect how trainers design, develop, and deliver training. Because people in your new employee orientation programs will vary greatly in educational background, life experiences, innate intelligence, and abilities, it's important to find out as much as possible about your participants before they attend the orientation session.

DIVERSITY ISSUES

Age Differences

One issue that comes up frequently in train-the-trainer and coaching courses relates to the effect of age on the learning process. Managers, supervisors, and trainers often say that older workers are "slower" and more difficult to train.

Just to set the record straight, researchers seem to be divided on the issue of age and one's ability to learn, depending on how one interprets "learning." In general, research on adult learning shows that adults continue to learn throughout the years, but they may take longer to learn new things. Although younger folks seem to be more efficient when it comes to memorizing information, older people are better able to evaluate and apply information.

Research shows that change in adulthood is a procession of critical periods during the 50-plus years following childhood and youth. Those periods comprise marked changes and experiences during which some of the most meaningful learning may occur.

Adults have a potential for continual learning and inquiry that conventional wisdom has sometimes failed to recognize. Researchers, however, do recognize that physical changes play a part in the learning process. As we age, we may experience some hearing loss, lower energy levels, and slower reaction time. Those factors should be taken into consideration, but they should not be regarded as proof that older people are slower or have greater difficulty learning. By observing and accommodating adult learning principles as well as basic concepts of individual differences, an instructor will be effective in training any adult.

The so-called generation gap seems to be widening more and more throughout the world and particularly in corporate America. At one end of the workplace continuum are the young professionals in their early 20s, and at the other end are the older employees for whom the idea of retirement is a fast-forming concept. The result is a much greater age gap in the workplace than ever before. The U.S. workforce is aging, and by the year 2005 those over 55 will make up 15 percent of the workforce.

Meeting the Training Needs of Older Employees

Although the ability to learn does not diminish with age, there are those who believe that anyone over 40 can't learn new skills. Such beliefs are bound to be reflected in the trainer's behavior in the classroom. Several studies show that people over 40 may take longer to learn new skills primarily because first they have to release the way they are currently doing things. For example, younger employees who have grown up with computers and video games will find it easier to learn new computer systems and software programs than their older colleagues who used typewriters throughout most of their careers.

One of the biggest barriers to older workers' learning new skills is their lack of confidence or fear of failure that is created, in part, by society's myths and stereotypes about aging. So the trainer's first challenge is to build older participants' confidence by encouraging them. Because some older adults experience a decline in vision or hearing, the trainer needs to pay attention to the room arrangement, lighting, and the use of larger print on visual aids and even in participant workbooks.

Those 35 and older are interested in receiving training that is relevant, immediately applicable, and presented in an easy-to-absorb format. Like the younger participants, those over 35 are in a hurry, but for different reasons. They realize that they must keep up and, in some cases, catch up to survive in today's fast-paced, high-pressured, and rapidly changing work environment.

Connecting with Younger Employees

Younger workers, the so-called "Generation Xers" (those born during the years 1965 to 1979) and "Gen Yers" (those born after 1979), present different challenges. Trainers as well as managers erroneously assume that these younger workers have short attention spans; are disrespectful, apathetic, and lazy; and think they know it all. The truth is that they are enthusiastic, confident, and achievement oriented. They can process large amounts of data at a time, but they want their information presented to them in abbreviated forms, such as sound bites and checklists. These characteristics create different challenges and opportunities for trainers in trying to meet the needs of this particular group.

In the classroom, give young participants many opportunities to apply their knowledge and solve problems through group discussion, simulations, case studies, and so forth. They like to be challenged and to receive immediate and meaningful feedback. Because they are easily bored, you need to design programs that offer a variety of learning experiences. The entertainment factor cannot be overlooked. Remember: This is the MTV generation. They expect high-quality materials, including participant workbooks, videos, and other visual aids.

Because they like to challenge as well as be challenged, they will question and demand proof of what you're saying. They will not accept your word at face value just because you're the trainer. Be prepared with facts and figures to support your statements and explain why they are learning a particular skill or piece of information, focusing particularly on outcomes and results. They do not like to be told what to do, so provide lots of opportunities for them to discover things on their own through structured experiences and self-assessment instruments.

Today's audiences, regardless of age, are conditioned by television, and consequently expect to take frequent "commercial breaks." This means that the training design must reflect the participants' need to get up and move around regularly or at least experience a change in venue or delivery methods.

Gender Differences

Gender issues continue to exist in corporate America and find their way into the corporate classroom. As a role model, you must demonstrate appropriate behavior at all times. For example, make sure task assignments are evenly distributed to both genders, preventing participants from falling into traditional roles, such as a woman recording and a man leading the discussion. You also must avoid making sexist remarks or using examples and activities that appeal more to one gender.

You can help bridge the gender gap by providing opportunities to heighten awareness of the different perspectives each gender brings to the same situation. You can promote this exchange of perspectives through small-group activities, making sure all groups include both men and women. During general discussions, solicit ideas and reactions from both men and women.

Culture

Today's corporate classroom is a patchwork of cultures. Cultural differences include ethnicity, race, gender, age, and chosen affiliations. People from different cultures can enrich the learning experience. You have a responsibility to understand and meet the learning needs of those whose experiences and frames of reference may be quite different from yours. It is our job to learn how to draw on the experience and background of these participants to add value to training, regardless of the topic. You also can create opportunities for participants from different backgrounds to learn about each other by working together in structured experiences. When choosing both methods and materials, you must make sure that you choose videos, case studies, and other activities that are inclusive and reflect your diverse audiences.

Make an effort to learn about the participants who come from other ethnic cultures by talking with them and asking them questions about their customs. Ask them for the correct pronunciation of their names and then practice that pronunciation. Address them correctly in class. You also can read articles and books about intercultural communication so that you are somewhat familiar with the cultures that are most frequently represented in your training sessions.

Keep in mind that, in many cultures, the approach to learning is very traditional. The instructor is considered an authority figure, and participants are expected to assume a passive role, with the trainer delivering content in a highly structured and rigid manner. As a result of their cultural conditioning, some people may be uncomfortable with a participative and interactive approach to learning. These participants may need a little more nudging and encouragement to increase their comfort level with the learning process. Co-operative learning techniques, such as asking them to discuss a question or problem in pairs or small groups, are effective ways of involving those who are not used to interactive learning.

Disabilities

Today's training audiences represent a variety of special needs and considerations. Some of your participants will have one or more disabilities. As with other differences, you must be sensitive to their situation and accommodate their special requirements, while remaining sensitive to their need to be treated just like everyone else.

You must learn to adapt your training methods and materials to accommodate the needs of participants with physical, mental, and even medical impairments. Find out in advance who may have special needs and accommodate those needs in the initial orientation program design.

For example, if a hearing-impaired person will be attending your session, you need to know if an interpreter will accompany the individual, or to what degree the participant can read lips. For a person who lip-reads, make sure the participant is seated so that he or she is able to see your face. You, of course, need to make sure that you turn toward that individual when speaking. When other participants respond to a question or make a comment, remind them to do the same, if possible.

Be sensitive to those who may have learning disabilities or literacy problems, or for whom English is a second language. Choose or create materials written at an appropriate reading level. This is where a presession questionnaire or other needs-assessment methods can be quite helpful.

I cannot overemphasize the importance of knowing as much as you can about the individuals who will be attending your session. Don't make assumptions about people just because they hold particular jobs or work at certain levels within the organization.

Provide written materials and write instructions for activities and exercises on a flipchart or transparency. Be sure to think through the logistics of your activities, keeping in mind your participants with special needs. Be aware that you cannot anticipate everything. No matter how well you plan, sometimes you will be caught off guard.

What to Do Next

◆ Read Chapter 3, "Designing an Interactive Program."

◆ Research the demographics of employees your organization has hired within the last 12 months. Then, based on that information, list the specific needs you should consider as you develop the program.

◆◆◆

The next chapter focuses on what makes an orientation program effective. It includes a discussion of the purpose and goals of an orientation program. It also addresses the various elements necessary for a successful program, such as topics, time allocation, and the involvement of key people in the process.

Designing an Interactive Program

What's in This Chapter?

- Purpose and goals of a new employee orientation program

- Elements of an effective program that addresses cognitive, affective, and behavioral learning domains

- Supervisor's preparation for the new employee's arrival

- What to cover on an employee's first day

- How to orient the new employee to the overall organization

Before you begin to design your new employee orientation program, you need to spend time upfront getting support, buy-in, and participation from others in the organization. You cannot design this program in a vacuum—you need to be clear about what the organization's top management wants to accomplish in a new employee orientation program. Of course, you can give them some guidance and direction by sharing what you already know about the needs of new employees and the goals of successful programs as identified in current research.

Purpose and Goals of the Program

The purposes and goals of a new employee orientation program are

- to provide employees with information that helps them integrate smoothly and quickly into the organization

- to introduce employees to the organization as a whole—its structure, philosophy, purpose, values, and so forth

- to help new employees identify the importance of their roles within the organization and how what they do affects others

- to introduce employees to their department's goals and their roles in helping meet those goals

- to promote communication between the employee and management

- to communicate expectations regarding policies, procedures, and performance

- to make new employees feel welcome and to assure them that they made the right decision in joining the team

- to get employees excited about being a part of the organization and motivated to do the best job possible.

In short, the program needs to be informative, motivational, and fun!

Elements of an Effective Orientation Program

For the orientation process to be successful, it must be established as a formal program with a program administrator. The training department is the most likely department to handle that responsibility. In addition to providing the basic framework for the program, the training department can be very helpful by conducting orientation training sessions for managers and supervisors. Such sessions should include

1. the purpose and objectives of an orientation program

2. the importance of orientation and its effects on performance and turnover

3. the supervisor's or manager's role

4. the benefits of proper orientation for the employee, the supervisor, and the company

5. checklists and manuals to help guide managers and supervisors through the orientation process

6. follow-up procedures.

Ideally, the orientation should provide an opportunity for the new employee to learn important information about the organization, and it should be conducted in a manner that incorporates adult learning principles and active training practices. For starters, be sure to kick off the formal orientation session with an icebreaker/mixer designed to create a comfortable environment and get people mixing and mingling quickly. Please don't use the old standby of going around the room and asking each person to do a self-introduction. It's boring, predictable, and awkward. Besides, after the first five or six people, no one is paying attention.

A new employee orientation program should be handled no differently than any other effective training design. It should include specific learning objectives, need-to-know rather than nice-to-know content, active training methods that focus on the participant and reflect adult learning principles, and ways to measure training effectiveness.

The design should address all three learning domains—cognitive, affective, and behavioral.

♦ **Cognitive learning** focuses on knowledge development, that is, the acquisition of information. In the case of our orientation program, we want participants to acquire knowledge about the organization, such as its history, culture, structure, philosophy, policies, and procedures.

♦ **Affective learning** addresses attitude development and deals with values or feelings. We want our new employees to feel good about their decision to join our organization and to get really excited about being part of the team. We also want them to embrace our corporate values and be sensitive to issues such as sexual harassment and diversity.

♦ **Behavioral learning** deals with skill development. It focuses on a person's being able to perform a task or procedure. This, of course, becomes particularly critical when the employee is actually on the job; however, the new employee orientation program should give participants an opportunity to learn how to complete forms, answer the telephone properly, use the organization's intranet system, operate the copier and fax machines, and so forth.

With those three learning domains in mind, the next step is to write specific, participant-centered learning objectives.

SETTING SPECIFIC LEARNING OBJECTIVES

Objectives serve as a type of contract. If participants know the program or session objectives at the beginning, they will know what they will be learning. Objectives give participants a sense of direction—what to expect from you and what you expect from them.

Clearly defined objectives serve as the basis for the design and development of the program—that is, the instructional plan. They help the trainer focus on desired outcomes and determine what the participants need to know and do in order to produce those outcomes.

Write objectives from the participant's point of view, not the trainer's. Put the emphasis not on what you want to cover but on what you want the participant to value, understand, or do with the subject, information, or skills when the training program is over.

At the end of the program use the objectives to evaluate the program's success. Because they describe what the participant will be able to do at the end of the training, the objectives automatically become the standard against which success is measured.

SELECTING THE PROGRAM CONTENT

When you have specified the learning objectives or outcomes, the next step is to decide what specific content should be included. During the first few weeks on the job, new employees are overwhelmed and it's tempting to want to give these folks everything at once. An effective orientation program will focus on what new employees *absolutely* need to know during the initial stages of their employment. Resist the "information-dump" approach that creates cognitive overload and results in a high level of participant frustration.

Content flows naturally from the learning objectives or outcomes. Content driven by the objectives should determine the length of the program. There are, however, a number of factors to consider that may be outside your control and may limit the amount of time available to you.

Because of the variables that enter into your decision about how long to make the program, I have designed both a one-day and a two-day module. To accommodate your various needs and constraints, both modules have built-in flexibility and choices of activities.

Standard Topics for a New Employee Orientation Program

Standard topics to cover fall into the following broad categories:

- Company history and context:

  - history

  - organization profile

- culture

- philosophy

- mission, vision, values

- goals and organization direction

- logo, tag line

- senior management team, department heads

- financial position

- locations, building layout

- structure

- products and services

- customers

- competitors

◆ Compensation and benefits:

- compensation, bonus

- insurance plans

- retirement, deferred compensation

- profit-sharing

- time off

- paid overtime

- workers' compensation

- tuition reimbursement

◆ Policies and procedures:

- work hours

- standards of personal conduct

- ethics

- safety

- ◆ emergencies

- ◆ computer and Internet usage

- ◆ sexual harassment

- ◆ parking

- ◆ attendance and tardiness

- ◆ rest and meal breaks

- ◆ performance evaluation

- ◆ Employee programs and services:

  - ◆ employee assistance program

  - ◆ mentoring

  - ◆ employee development

  - ◆ service and recognition awards.

CHOOSING STRATEGIES AND METHODS

When you have identified *what* you are going to include in the program, the next step is to determine *how* you are going to communicate that content. Instructional methods are the various means by which content or material is communicated. They include the use of activities (structured experiences) and a variety of cooperative-learning or active-training techniques.

The designs in this workbook reflect the underlying philosophy that adult participants need to be involved actively throughout the training session. The design and development strategies, therefore, offer an active, experiential approach to training, allowing participants to discover ideas, principles, and concepts through a series of well-planned and well-executed activities. Because the adult, in particular, learns by doing, not by being told, these designs include very few didactic elements.

Setting the Tone for Supervisors

The success or failure of a training session often is determined long before the first participant sets foot in the training room. The new employee orientation program is no exception, particularly because the orientation program is a process, not a one-time event.

Orienting the new employee should begin even before that worker's first day on the job. It's important for the employee's supervisor to make a personal telephone contact, welcoming the new person to the organization. Every effort should be made to make him or her feel like a part of the team.

The following checklists, sample memos, and other tools located in chapter 11 will be helpful to supervisors, in particular, in preparing for the new employee's arrival:

- ◆ Tool 11–2: Sample Memo to the New Employee's Co-workers (page 178 or *Tool 11–2.pdf* on the CD)

- ◆ Tool 11–3: Tasks to Do Before the New Employee's First Day (page 180 or *Tool 11–3.pdf* on the CD)

- ◆ Tool 11–5: New Employee's Work Area Preparation Checklist (page 184 or *Tool 11–5.pdf* on the CD)

- ◆ Tool 11–7: Information to Communicate During the New Employee's First Day (page 188 or *Tool 11–7.pdf* on the CD)

- ◆ Tool 11–8: Suggested First-Day Work-Related Assignments (page 190 or *Tool 11–8.pdf* on the CD).

First Day—New Employee Concerns

Orienting a new employee goes beyond the company's formal orientation program. It is important that the new employee feels comfortable in his or her new surroundings, whether at an executive or an entry level, whether new to the company or to the department. The new employee's comfort should be a primary consideration, and it is the manager's or supervisor's responsibility to aid the employee's adaptation to the work environment.

The first day is critical to the employee's success and for that reason should be planned and orchestrated very carefully. New employees are filled with anxiety and confusion. In short, they are overwhelmed. They begin to question the decision they made. Did I do the right thing? Am I really qualified to do this job? Will I like my boss and the people I work with? Will I fit in? The way in which a person is treated on his or her first day will determine whether that person's fears and anxieties are warranted and, as a result, how he or she will approach this new experience.

Managers and supervisors need to take care of the basics—help the employee adjust quickly so he or she can concentrate on doing what he or she was hired to do. Failure to orient the employee properly will result in poor attitude, low morale and productivity, performance problems, and, in some cases, the loss of a valuable worker. The sooner an employee adapts and feels comfortable, the sooner he or she becomes productive. Even before the employee walks into the work area, efforts should be made to help him or her feel part of the organization and see himself or herself as part of the team.

Begin by taking a look at the employee's immediate needs and concerns and putting yourself in his or her shoes. Think back to your first day on the job. How did you feel? What were your concerns and expectations? What did you want and need to know?

New employees also have certain wants and expectations. They want to be treated humanely and respectfully. They want to know what is expected of them and how they will go about learning their new jobs. They want to know how they fit into the total picture and how they will be rewarded. We tend to overlook or forget the fact that people begin a job with success in mind; they genuinely want to do a good job. This commitment and enthusiasm is either squelched or encouraged within the first few hours on the job.

A manager or supervisor will be on target in addressing the new employee's concerns if he or she approaches orientation from the basic who, what, where, when, why, and how questions.

Who
- is senior management?
- can I go to for help?
- do I report to?
- do I interact with?

What
- are the job requirements?
- are the manager's expectations?
- are the standards of performance?
- are the policies and procedures regarding
    - smoking
    - dress
    - sickness
    - vacation

- coffee pot
- lunch room clean-up
- parties
- call-in
- travel and expense reports?

◆ is the structure of the department?

◆ advancement/development opportunities are available to me?

Where ◆ should I park?

◆ will I find

- restrooms
- the lunch area
- my work area
- the employee lounge
- supplies
- equipment
- reference material
- files and records?

When ◆ do I go to lunch and take breaks?

◆ will I be paid?

◆ will I be evaluated?

◆ should I report for work each day?

◆ can I expect to leave each day?

Why ◆ do we follow that procedure?

◆ do I have to do this?

How ◆ do I operate the

- telephone

- ◆ photocopier

- ◆ fax machine

- ◆ postage meter

- ◆ computer/word processor?

- ◆ do I fit into this department?

- ◆ will I be trained?

- ◆ will I be evaluated?

- ◆ will I be compensated for overtime?

- ◆ do I process the mail?

- ◆ do I order supplies?

- ◆ do I use email?

Chapter 8, "Conducting a Departmental Orientation," will provide you with various ideas and strategies for assimilating the new employee into the organization's culture and the actual work environment.

Organization-Level Orientation

Within three to six weeks, the employee should attend an organization-level orientation that addresses the company's history, philosophy, culture, goals, and direction. The purpose is to introduce employees to the organization as a whole and help them feel a part of it. This is also a good opportunity to elaborate on career opportunities and emphasize the importance of each person's role to the success of the organization. Members of senior management should participate as guest speakers, preferably in person or, at the very least, through a videotape.

It's a nice touch to host a short reception during a break or after the session during which members of management mingle with the newcomers, getting to know them on a personal level and answering any questions they were afraid to ask in front of the group.

Depending on the size of the organization, "Breakfast with the President" might be another element of the orientation process. In that program, the president or another senior manager meets with groups of 10 to 12 employees who have been on the job approximately three months. The senior member solicits feedback and answers employees' questions about the organization as a whole. This is a good opportunity to identify and address potential problems before they become major issues and to help remove some of the mystique employees often associate with senior management.

Participant Materials

Printed materials are an important element of a new employee orientation program. Each participant should receive a three-ring binder with the following materials and corresponding tab dividers:

- mission, vision, values

- organization history

- organization structure

- products and services

- employee handbook

- resources and contacts

- helpful information

- "fun stuff."

Some of the information will already be in the binders when they are distributed to the participants at the beginning of the program; other materials will be added throughout the program.

It's also a nice touch to include organization mementos, such as logo pens, pins, mugs, and product samples. You might include the annual report, brochures, and maps. Create a fun, practical, and professional package that also can serve as an important and useful reference.

Creating the Environment

One of the major underlying goals of the new employee orientation program is to make it enjoyable and to show new employees how much we value them. To that end, put the time, energy, and money into making the actual training session a memorable experience. One way to accomplish this is by establishing a theme and creating the physical environment that reflects it.

For example, you might choose a cruise ship theme. The cruise ship becomes the metaphor for the organization and throwing a Bon Voyage party celebrates the beginning of the cruise. In effect, the new employees are celebrating the beginning of their new job and career opportunity. At the door to the training room, post a sign that reads, "Welcome Aboard the *SS [company name]*." Greet each new employee with a Hawaiian lei and a Welcome Aboard packet of materials, including some "fun stuff." Decorate the room with streamers and balloons. Play party music and have each new employee pose for a picture as he or she enters the room (just like people do on a real cruise ship). And you will have to have food! When the new employees are "onboard" you can "set sail" for their exciting journey. You can expand the metaphor to include "ports of call" (learning about various departments) and "life rafts" (various resources to contact with questions). Try out other themes, such as outer space, the old west, races, or sports events. Let your imagination and creativity run wild.

What to Do Next

- ◆ Meet with senior managers, department heads, supervisors, and newer employees to discuss goals and objectives of the program.

- ◆ Determine the content with input from those key people.

- ◆ Determine the length of the program that is required to meet stated goals and objectives.

- ◆ Create a preliminary design.

- ◆ Make decisions regarding learning activities and experiences.

- ◆ Contact key people and subject matter experts who can participate as facilitators and presenters.

◆ ◆ ◆

Now that you have the "big-picture" perspective of an effective new employee orientation program, the next step is to focus on some of the specifics. The following chapter includes tasks and timelines you need to address as you prepare for your program.

Preparing for a New Employee Orientation Program

What's in This Chapter?

- Timeline for program preparation actions

- General lists of facilitator and participant materials and equipment

- Explanation of facilitator's principal responsibilities during the orientation

- Discussion of questioning techniques and feedback

The better prepared you are, the more effective you will be in facilitating this new employee orientation program. This chapter offers some tips to help you deliver a dynamic and successful program.

Preparing for the Program

FACILITATOR'S TIMELINE

One month prior to the session:

- Send invitation and schedule memo to participants.

- Send invitation to guest facilitators.

- Send memo to participants' managers.

- Schedule training room.

- Order refreshments.

Two to four weeks prior to the session:

- Send confirmation to participants along with any presession material, such as background reading.

- Obtain necessary equipment and materials.

- Begin preparing for the program.

- Meet with guest facilitators.

One week prior to the session:

- Assemble participant and instructor materials, including handouts and slides.

- Double-check participant registration.

The day before the session:

- Double-check all materials.

- Check on room set-up.

- Review your program; conduct your own dress rehearsal.

- Check equipment operability.

FACILITATOR MATERIALS

- Facilitator's guide

- Copies of helpful tools (chapters 10 and 11) and activity handouts (chapter 10)

- Slides

- Markers for flipchart and transparencies

- Masking tape

- Reference material

- Paper

- Pen or pencil

- Clock

PARTICIPANT MATERIALS

- Pencils or pens

- Paper

- Tent cards

- Black wide-tipped markers

- Post-it notes

- Binder, notebook, or folder for handouts

- Organization materials (brochures, maps, employee handbook, and so forth)

FACILITIES AND EQUIPMENT

- One table (round, oval, or square) for every four participants and an appropriate number of participant chairs

- One flipchart and extra pad (for facilitator)

- One flipchart for every four participants

- LCD projector and screen

- Extension cord

- VCR and video recorder (optional)

- Table for training materials

- Table for refreshments

- Cups, glasses, napkins, as needed

- Water pitchers and glasses

FACILITATOR PREPARATION

- Make copies of handouts (one for each participant).

- Prepare PowerPoint slides.

- Prepare flipchart pages for Learning Activity 10–6: What Do You Want to Know?" (chapter 10, page 109). At the top of each page, write your subtopics (for example, Benefits, Company History, Organization Structure/Departments, Products/Services). With masking tape, post these pages in order on the walls of your meeting room.

Refreshments

Providing coffee, tea, fruit, and pastries is a great way to begin each morning session, and fruit juice, snacks, and soda served during the afternoon break help keep energy levels up and help establish and maintain rapport. To promote group cohesion and keep the session on track, I recommend that lunch be provided on-site.

Breaks

Schedule one 15-minute break midmorning and another midafternoon. Depending on the group, however, you may wish to take two breaks both morning and afternoon.

Facilitator Responsibilities

As the program facilitator, you have the following primary responsibilities:

- **Role model.** Participants will look to you to set the tone and model appropriate behaviors. In other words, it's important that you practice what you preach.

- **Discussion guide.** You must lead the discussion and encourage everyone's participation. Remember that one definition of *facilitate* is "to make easier."

- **Keeper of the agenda.** It is important not to lose track of program objectives. You must be the guardian of the agenda. Use it to limit griping sessions and redirect tangents. After giving a maximum of 10 minutes to them, say something like, "That's an interesting point. However, it's important that we get back on track so we can achieve our program objectives." To maintain the agenda and keep participants focused,

  - start on time

  - stick to the agenda

  - maintain group involvement

  - control the discussion

◆ give feedback

◆ summarize frequently.

Using Questioning Techniques

Questions increase group participation. Discussion generated by the questions will help participants share their knowledge and experience. You'll find that questions have been suggested for many of the activities in this workbook. However, at times you will want to add your own questions. Remember to use open-ended questions beginning with "How..." or "Tell me..." to elicit opinions and encourage the sharing of ideas. Other key words in questions include *when, where, which,* and *what.* Use *why* sparingly because it tends to put people on the defensive.

When a question meets with blank stares, use one or more of the following suggestions to prompt discussion:

◆ Rephrase the question.

◆ Call on a specific person—someone you know will have a response.

◆ Quickly separate participants into small groups. Ask them to discuss the question among themselves and arrive at a group answer.

◆ Answer the question yourself. (Try not to do this too often.)

◆ Go on to your next point or question and come back to the initial question a little later.

Providing Feedback

The ability to listen and respond effectively is one of the trainer's most important skills. Providing feedback (that is, commenting on what is said) can reinforce a particular point, enhance a participant's self-esteem, and encourage further discussion. Listen to what a participant says and comment on his or her ideas before going on to another person's ideas. Be encouraging, with phrases such as, "That's a good point," or "Your point is very important" when someone participates. Be sure to provide feedback during general discussions as well as after simulation activities.

Glossary of Terms

The following terms are commonly used in the training profession and will be helpful in preparing you for your training assignment.

Facilitation—The process by which the trainer guides group discussion

Icebreaker/opening activity—An activity used at the beginning of a program to lessen participant anxiety

Lecturette—Prepared background material delivered verbally to the group

Program—Term used to describe the interactive, experiential learning process; synonymous with "workshop"

Facilitating Small-Group Activities

Prepare the group by writing brief and specific instructions on a flipchart. Explain where they are to gather, what they are to do, and how much time they are allotted. During the activity, circulate among the groups and sit or kneel for a few minutes with each to check their progress. Provide a two-minute warning near the end of the allotted time so that groups can arrive at conclusions on time.

What to Do Next

◆ Develop your own timeline and task list as described in this chapter.

◆ Create participant and facilitator materials checklists for your program, based on your preliminary thoughts and the information in this chapter.

◆ Read chapter 5, "Facilitating a New Employee Orientation Program."

◆◆◆

Regardless of the length and content of your program, it's important that you have an understanding of what you need to do to make the content come alive during the actual session. The next chapter introduces you to tips and techniques for facilitating an interactive program.

Facilitating a New Employee Orientation Program

What's in This Chapter?

- How facilitators differ from presenters

- Nonverbal and verbal ways to encourage participation

- Tips for responding to questions

- Tips for dealing with challenging situations and participants

Standing up in front of a group and presenting information is one thing; facilitating discussion and participant interaction is another. Each endeavor requires a different skill set. If you accept the changing role of the trainer—from "teacher" to "facilitator"—then you will have to understand and develop facilitation skills.

Anytime you work *with* a group in a participant-centered environment instead of talking *at* that group, you are facilitating the learning process. Facilitation skills are particularly critical when you process or debrief activities because the debriefing session is where the real learning takes place.

Ways to Encourage Participation

Your behavior throughout the session sends a message that either encourages or discourages participation. Sometimes the messages are pretty straightforward; sometimes they are much more subtle. Those subtle messages, often communicated without our awareness, can have a very powerful effect.

Material in this chapter was adapted from The Trainer's Handbook *by Karen Lawson (San Francisco: Jossey-Bass/Pfeiffer, 1998).*

NONVERBAL COMMUNICATION

What you *do* often speaks more loudly than what you *say*. Use the power of these nonverbal communication techniques to encourage participation:

- **Eye contact.** Be attentive to the group by making eye contact with all participants.

- **Head nodding.** Nod your head to show understanding and encourage the participant to continue with his or her comments or questions.

- **Posture.** Avoid defensive postures, such as folded arms. Be aware of your body language. For example, when you need to point to someone, do so with an open palm, not with your finger.

- **Body movement.** Avoid distracting movements, such as too much walking and pacing. Move toward people to draw them into the discussion.

- **Smiling.** Concentrate on smiling to encourage and relax the group.

VERBAL COMMUNICATION

What you say and how you say it may shut down or may encourage participation. Always be mindful of the difference between intent and perception. Frequently conduct your own reality check by asking yourself, "What is my intent, and how am I being perceived?" Keep in mind that many new employees will be feeling anxious or overwhelmed. If so, they may be reluctant to speak up. It is, therefore, even more critical that you, as the facilitator, do your best to involve and engage each participant. In general discussions, practice using the following techniques to create an exciting and positive learning environment.

- **Praise or Encourage.** Use simple, but powerful, words of encouragement to prod the participant to continue:

  - "I'm glad you brought that up."

  - "Tell me more."

  - "Okay, let's build on that."

  - "Good point. Who else has an idea?"

  - "I would like to hear your thoughts about. . . ."

◆ **Accept or Use Participants' Ideas.** Clarify, build on, and further develop ideas suggested by participants:

- ◆ "To piggyback on your point, Juan. . . ."

- ◆ "As Salina mentioned earlier. . . ."

◆ **Accept Participants' Feelings.** Use statements that communicate acceptance of and willingness to clarify feelings:

- ◆ "I sense that you are upset by what I just said."

- ◆ "You seem to feel very strongly about this issue."

- ◆ "I know it's hard to maintain a positive outlook when you are at risk of being a downsizing casualty."

- ◆ "I can imagine that you feel. . . ."

THE ART OF QUESTIONING

The art of asking questions is central to your success as a facilitator of adult learning. The key, however, is to ask questions that stimulate discussion and interaction rather than questions that elicit simple factual responses reminiscent of teacher–student question-and-answer exchanges in primary school. To stimulate discussion, be sure your questions are open-ended.

People often think they are asking open-ended questions when they are not. An open-ended question is one that begins with *who, what, where, when, why,* or *how* because those words will elicit more detailed and meaningful responses from your participants. Closed-ended questions, on the other hand, are questions that can be answered with a simple "yes" or "no." They do not encourage participation.

To make this easy, try to ask questions that begin with *how* or *what.* If you can get into the habit of asking those kinds of questions, your group discussions and processing segments will be very effective. Avoid using questions that begin with *why* because they imply a need for the answerer to justify his or her position. They can put people on the defensive.

When you have asked a question, be quiet. Trainers tend to ask a question and if no one responds immediately, they answer the question themselves. Silence is uncomfortable, but don't feel you have to speak up and fill the void. Let silence happen. Be silent for 10 to 12 seconds to give people time to think of their responses. If you keep answering your own questions, there is no reason for participants to offer their ideas.

Responding to Participants' Questions

In a lively, risk-free, and dynamic environment, participants will be stimulated to ask questions as well as to answer them. Although this certainly is what we want to happen, this type of participant interaction can be quite challenging for the trainer. To help you master the art of responding to questions, consider the following guidelines.

SET THE GROUND RULES AT THE BEGINNING

At the beginning of the session, explain to the participants how you are going to handle questions. You can offer to take questions throughout the session, you can stop at intervals and solicit questions, or you can ask participants to hold questions until the end. Because the program is interactive instead of didactic, questions probably will be minimal and likely will surface during the debriefing of the activity. Sometimes you will need to limit the number of questions or the time spent addressing them in order to stay on schedule. The important thing is to communicate clearly when you will and won't take questions. You might suggest that if a question comes to mind during the session, the participant should write it down so it isn't forgotten.

REPEAT THE QUESTION

Trainers should make a habit of repeating or paraphrasing a question before answering it. By repeating the question, you accomplish three things:

1. You ensure that the group has heard the question.

2. You check to see that you have heard the question correctly.

3. You buy yourself a little time to organize your thoughts before answering.

To ensure that the question received is the same as the one intended, paraphrase the question by saying, "If I heard you correctly, your question is. . . . Is that right?" If the question is long, ask if you may reword it, then restate it concisely and check to see that you have captured its essence. Be careful, however, not to paraphrase using any of these phrases:

◆   "What you mean is . . . ."

- ◆ "What you're saying is . . . ."

- ◆ "What you're trying to say is . . . ."

Such words are insulting and condescending. Their subtle message is, "You're obviously not articulate in expressing yourself, so let me help you out."

USE EYE CONTACT

Look directly at the person who asked the question while you are paraphrasing. When you deliver your response, direct it to the entire group, not only to the person who asked the question.

CHOOSE YOUR WORDS CAREFULLY

Think about the effect your words may have on individual participants. Avoid using words like *obviously,* which implies that the person asking the question should already know the answer. Along the same line, avoid phrases such as "You have to understand. . . ," which comes across as ordering and directing, and "You should. . . ," which may be received as preaching or moralizing.

RESPECT THE GROUP

Never belittle or embarrass a participant, even when you have to exercise a little patience because someone asks a question that you have already addressed in your presentation. Absolutely never say, "As I already mentioned. . . ." Instead, answer the question by carefully rewording your point so that you are not repeating the remark exactly as you said it earlier.

RESPOND TO INDIVIDUAL CONCERNS

Sometimes a participant will ask a question that is quite narrowly focused and pertains only to the person asking it. If that happens, give a brief response and then suggest that the two of you talk about it after the session. Use this same strategy with those who ask questions unrelated to the topic. Always indicate your openness and willingness to talk further one-on-one. Above all else, you want to project compassion and concern.

COVER ALL PARTS OF THE ROOM

Some trainers look only to their right or to their left, and so entertain questions from only one side of the room. Although their directional tendency is unconscious, people on the side being ignored will become anxious and annoyed. Similarly, some trainers will acknowledge only participants who are seated in the front because it's easy to see and hear them. Make a concerted effort to take questions from all parts of the audience.

DON'T BLUFF

People may ask questions that you can't answer. Be honest. Don't be afraid to say, "I don't know." But don't leave it at that. Offer to check further and get back to them by phone or mail or at a later session. You also might tell them where they can get the additional information themselves.

WHAT NOT TO SAY

In an effort to be supportive and encouraging, trainers will often respond to a participant by saying, "That's a good question." The danger here is that you may come across as patronizing or insincere. And questioners who do not receive the same feedback or reinforcement may feel their questions weren't as good. Instead, comment by saying, "That's an interesting question" or "That's an intriguing question." Similarly, telling a questioner "I'm glad you asked that question" may leave others feeling that you aren't glad they asked a question.

After delivering your response, don't say, "Does that answer your question?" What happens if the participant responds that you didn't answer the question? Worse still, the participant may not have had his or her question answered but doesn't want to embarrass you or himself or herself, and just lets it go. By asking if you answered the question, you give up some control and you suggest a lack of confidence in your answer. A better response would be, "What other questions do you have?" or "Would you like me to go into more detail?"

Dealing with Problem Situations

No matter how well you have planned and prepared for your program, more often than not, you will be faced with the unexpected. What starts out as a terrific session can become your worst nightmare. Some human behavior, attitudes, or reactions are predictable. It's your job as a trainer to anticipate these behaviors, prevent them if you can, and if not, deal with them effectively.

One useful tool for keeping the session on track is the Parking Lot. Post a flipchart page with the words *Parking Lot* at the top. Give participants pads of Post-it notes and explain that if issues unrelated to the topic come up during the session, they may be asked to jot them down on the Post-its and put them in the "parking lot." This technique allows participants to acknowledge their issues and concerns and get them out of the way. The technique gives you a way to keep things on track by saying, "Your point is well taken, although it's not relevant to what we're talking about now. I suggest you write it down and put it in the parking lot, and we'll be sure to address it before the end of the session."

KEEP YOUR COOL

When faced with the unexpected, the most important thing to remember is to maintain your composure. You must remain calm and in control. Several techniques will help you in such situations:

- ◆ **Lower your pitch.** When we get nervous or upset, our vocal pitch tends to rise, particularly for women. Pay attention to the sound of your voice.

- ◆ **Breathe deeply.** Shallow breathing is a sign of nervousness and will affect the quality of your voice. Deep breathing will calm you.

- ◆ **Control your speed.** Many people speak faster when they are under stress, so concentrate on maintaining a moderate rate of speech.

- ◆ **Control your volume.** Although you want to project your voice, don't yell. Maintain a reasonable volume level, loud enough to make sure you're heard but not so loud that you sound angry or out of control.

- ◆ **Attend to nonverbals.** Avoid nervous gestures such as fiddling with clothes, jewelry, paper clips, pointer, and so forth. Those are dead giveaways that you are losing control. Also, be careful not to appear in a counterattack mode. For example, if you are gesturing, keep your palms open and don't point.

HANDLE CHALLENGES WITH GRACE AND PROFESSIONALISM

Accept the fact that you are not always going to be correct. If someone points out an error and you believe that person is correct, thank the individual for pointing it out to you. Whatever you do, don't get defensive. An individual may challenge you by offering a different opinion or point of view. When that happens, acknowledge the difference of opinion and thank the person for offering a different point of view. Don't, however, get into an argument or a debate.

People automatically ask questions that start with *why.* Quite naturally, you may feel challenged and have a tendency to react defensively. To avoid delivering a defensive-sounding response, first reframe the *why* into a *how* or *what* question when you restate it. For example, if someone poses the question, "Why did you...?" you could reframe it by saying, "If I understand you correctly, you're asking me *how* I...." Or, "As I understand it, you want to know *what* I...." When responding to these challenging questions, begin with the phrase, "In my experience...," or present facts or quote experts as appropriate.

Side conversations are a frequent and annoying occurrence. Far too often, two or more members of the group engage in their own conversation while fellow participants are and/or the presenter is talking. You might need to try more than one strategy to bring them back. Sometimes just walking over to the people involved will cause them to stop their conversation. If that doesn't work, try saying, "[persons' names], we were just talking about.... What are your thoughts about that?"

Dealing with Problem Participants

More often than not, the group as a whole is not a problem but there may be a few difficult people in your new employee orientation session. The following are some coping strategies for dealing with specific character types.

THE TALKATIVE TYPE

The talkative participant has something to say about everything. This person always volunteers to be a group leader, to answer questions, or to offer suggestions. He or she seems to want to be the center of attention. To deal with the talkative type, you might say something like, "I appreciate your contribution, but let's hear from some other people." You also might suggest further discussion at break or lunch by saying, "In order to stay on schedule and on track, let's discuss this further during the break or after the session."

THE SILENT TYPE

Every group has one or more silent members. This person seems attentive and alert but will not volunteer comments or answer questions. He or she may be naturally shy or uncomfortable speaking up in a group and seems content just to listen.

You might ask yourself, "So what's wrong with that?" The problem is that often these quiet people have some wonderful comments and ideas to contribute, and if we don't make an effort to involve them, their ideas never surface and the group misses the opportunity to learn from another of its members. The participant himself or herself misses the chance to be heard and receive validation. Try prompting the reluctant or shy participant by saying, "[person's name], I know you have some experience in this area from your previous employment. It would be helpful if you would share your thoughts with the group." Another approach is to separate the group into pairs or trios. The shy person is much more likely to participate in smaller groups.

THE CLUELESS ATTENDEE

This person seems to have no idea what's going on. He or she totally misunderstands the question or the topic being discussed and gives answers or makes remarks that don't relate even remotely to the subject under discussion. To this person say, "Something I said must have led you off track. What I was trying to say is. . . ."

THE RAMBLER

This person talks on and on about nothing. He or she digresses frequently and uses examples and analogies that don't relate to the topic being discussed. This person is different from the clueless individual in that the rambler knows what's going on but prefers to follow his or her own agenda. To get this person back on track, try saying, "I don't understand. How does this relate to what we're talking about?" This is a good opportunity to use the Parking Lot.

THE BELLIGERENT PERSON

This person is openly hostile, challenging and arguing every point. He or she questions the presenter's knowledge and credibility and may even accuse the presenter of being out of touch with the real world. Whatever you do, don't engage in any verbal sparring. Say to this person, "I understand and appreciate your point of view. What do some of the rest of you think?" By turning to the rest of the group, you get yourself off the hook and give others an opportunity to exert some peer pressure to change this person's behavior. You might also offer to discuss the issue further during break.

THE KNOW-IT-ALL

The know-it-all tries to upstage or overshadow the facilitator. Often viewing himself or herself as an authority on every subject, this person assumes a superior role with both the group and the presenter. He or she relishes the opportunity to flaunt knowledge, use big words, quote facts and figures, and drop names. Although it's difficult, don't let your annoyance show. Acknowledge his or her contribution by saying, "That's one point of view. However, there are other ways of looking at it." Depending on the situation, you might ask other participants for their opinions or you may choose to move on.

THE NEGATIVE PERSON

We would expect that a new employee would not display any negative behavior. If the employee has been on the job for several weeks, however, he or she may have had an unpleasant experience already or may have become a bit disenchanted with the position or the organization. If so, he or she may complain about the organization, the boss, co-workers, anything. In addition to the negative verbal remarks, he or she displays negative nonverbal behavior, such as frowning or assuming a defensive posture. This person often is a chronic complainer who has nothing positive to contribute. Say something like, "I understand your point. What suggestions do you have to change the situation?" Or you might say, "For the sake of discussion, what might be some arguments for the opposite point of view?"

THE INDIFFERENT ATTENDEE

It's pretty clear to you and the rest of the group that this person does not want to be there. He or she makes no attempt to participate or contribute, perhaps believing that an orientation session is an unnecessary waste of time. Because he or she has been forced to attend, this person not only shows no interest but also may engage in his or her own activities separate from the group. Use a tactic similar to the one you might use with a silent person: "I know you have some experience in this area. Please tell us. . . ."

PEOPLE WHOSE PERSONALITIES CLASH

You may have two or more people who just don't get along. They engage in verbal battle, directly or indirectly, often with very personal and hurtful remarks. When a situation like that occurs, it is important to address it early by invoking your ground rules or saying, "I suggest that we keep personalities out of the discussion. Let's get back to the topic at hand."

General Guidelines

When dealing with any challenging situation or participant, keep in mind four important goals:

1. **Stop the dysfunctional behavior.** Your first objective is to get the person or persons to stop their disruptive behavior.

2. **Keep the individual(s) engaged.** Your second objective is to prevent the person from shutting down and not participating at all.

3. **Keep the rest of the group involved.** Your third objective is to prevent others in the group from shutting down. Remember that others will judge you by the way you handle difficult situations.

4. **Respect the individual.** Your fourth objective, and perhaps the most important, is to respect the person and help maintain his or her dignity. Whatever you do, don't embarrass or belittle anyone.

When you have addressed a behavior or responded to a hostile participant, look to another person or section of the audience. Continued eye contact will only further encourage the participant and may result in a continued debate or argument. Remember that you can never win an argument with a participant. Even if the group is annoyed with their fellow participant's behavior, if you attack that person, the others may turn against you. After all, he or she is one of them.

When participants demonstrate intense negative emotions, it's important to acknowledge those feelings and emotions with a statement like, "I can tell you feel strongly about this" or "I'm sorry you feel that way." Be careful not to make judgmental statements like, "You're being negative" or "You're not listening."

Learning to Live with What You Encounter

One of the biggest challenges you may face is to accept the fact that you can't control some people and some situations. When, despite all your efforts, the session still does not go according to plan, assess the situation as objectively as possible. Ask yourself what you could have done differently. If you conclude that you did everything you could to prevent or handle the situation, then don't dwell on it. If you think you could have handled the situation better, then learn from your mistakes and move on.

What to Do Next

◆ Think about any problem situations you might encounter and how you will handle them.

◆ Review the activities you are going to facilitate. Anticipate questions participants might ask and prepare your responses.

◆ Share these facilitation tips with guest facilitators.

◆ Read chapter 6, "Evaluating Your New Employee Orientation Program."

◆ ◆ ◆

Although you may not have developed your orientation program at this point, it's not too early to think about how you are going to evaluate its effectiveness. The following chapter introduces various ways to measure the value of the program to the new employee as well as to the organization.

Evaluating Your New Employee Orientation Program

What's in This Chapter?

* Three reasons to evaluate your new employee orientation program

* Kirkpatrick's four-level model for evaluating training

* Methods for capturing assessment information

How many times have you heard someone say, "It was a great training program but . . . "? Unfortunately, that statement (or some variation) is spoken far too often and reflects a growing concern by both line managers and senior management that training is costly and not always worth the investment of time and money. This particularly may be true as it relates to a new employee orientation program. Line managers may believe that the employee's time is better spent learning the job at his or her work site, not in a one-day or two-day session off-site learning information that could be acquired by reading the employee handbook or accessing the company's intranet.

This chapter will help you identify and use various methods to measure the value of the new employee orientation program so that you can gain greater commitment from managers at all levels of the organization.

Purposes of Evaluation

There are three reasons to evaluate your new employee orientation program:

1. **Determine whether the training achieved its objectives.**
   Based on your discussion with key people in your organization, you set the goals and objectives for the program. Evaluation is the only way to determine if those goals and objectives were met.

2. **Assess the value of the orientation program.** You will want to know the effect the program has on the employee's satisfaction with the organization and how quickly he or she is able to adapt to the environment and to the job itself.

3. **Identify program areas that need improvement.** Evaluation will help you identify what works and what doesn't so that you can adapt your design accordingly, always striving for improvement. It also will help you identify topics that need more emphasis and perhaps others more appropriately delivered through another medium.

What to Evaluate

Before you develop an evaluation process, you need to be clear about what you want to evaluate. This is not as easy as it might seem. Do you want to know what the participants thought about the program and about you? Do you want to evaluate how much the participants have learned? Do you want to find out if the information is helping participants on the job? Do you want to know if this structured approach to new employee orientation is making a difference to the organization?

FOUR-LEVEL MODEL FOR EVALUATING TRAINING

The most widely known model for evaluating training programs was introduced by Donald Kirkpatrick in 1959. It is regarded as a classic by training practitioners. Although all four levels of the model (reaction, learning, behavior, results) are important, you may choose not to evaluate at all four levels. Studies show that a vast majority of organizations evaluate reaction. A significantly high percentage measures learning as well. The evaluation or measurement of behavior lags behind the first two levels, and results are measured least often.

Level 1: Reaction

Level 1 deals with participant reaction, that is, "customer" satisfaction. Level 1 evaluations are often referred to as "smile sheets," which implies that participants' reactions are based on how much "fun" they had in the training session. Gauging reactions is an important first step in determining the success of a training program because reactions can help you determine the effectiveness of a program and how it can be improved. Kirkpatrick believed that you cannot bypass this first level because, as he put it, "If they [participants] do not react favorably, they will not be motivated to learn" (Kirkpatrick, 1994).

What Level 1 Can't Measure

One of the problems with and the main cause of criticism of Level 1 evaluation is that it is too subjective and often becomes nothing more than a popularity contest. Before you start constructing a participant end-of-program evaluation form, you must understand what that evaluation cannot and is not intended to do. It does not measure learning or the ability to apply learning on the job. It also cannot measure changes in attitudes or beliefs. Because this level deals only with participants' perceptions and reactions, a Level 1 instrument cannot measure organizational impact. Also, although the question frequently is found as a line item on participant sheets, participants cannot measure the trainer's knowledge. Think about it: How could the participants have any way of knowing what the trainer does and does not know about the subject? The trainer's ability to *communicate* or *demonstrate* his or her knowledge is an entirely different matter.

Deciding What to Measure at Level 1

Before you design a Level 1 instrument, you must be clear about what you want to know, why you want to know it, and what are you going to do with the information. Don't ask for information about something you can't change or have no intention of analyzing or reporting.

Designing an End-of-Program Evaluation Form

When you have identified the issues you want to measure, you then create questions or response items that address or fall into many, if not all, of the following categories:

- ◆ content
- ◆ materials
- ◆ instructional methods
- ◆ trainer
- ◆ environment
- ◆ logistics.

It is also a good idea to provide an opportunity for respondents to recommend ways in which the program may be improved and to express their overall reactions to the session.

I have included a sample end-of-program questionnaire designed to evaluate participant reaction. You will find this questionnaire (Handout 10–12) on page 172 or you can insert the accompanying CD and open the file titled *Handout 10–12.pdf.*

Conducting Interviews

You can use interviews to increase the reliability of the data collected from the questionnaires. This method of data collection is quite flexible, enabling the interviewer to probe for more specific answers and to clarify questions as needed. The interviewer can record spontaneous answers to get a more complete picture of the participants' reactions, and can explore in greater detail the reactions gleaned from the questionnaires.

Plan on spending about 30 minutes per interview. From a practical point, you will not be able to interview every participant. Instead, select a random sample of participants to interview. Hold the interviews within one week of the session so that the experience is fresh in their minds. Through one-on-one interviews, you can explore the reasons for participants' reactions and solicit suggestions for improvement. You may either tape the interviews and have them transcribed (thus enabling you to analyze or interpret the responses more thoroughly) or simply take notes during the interview.

When developing the interview questions, do not duplicate the questions on the written form. Instead, ask specific questions about the methods used or the content covered. For example, here are several questions you could ask about the methods used in the new employee orientation session:

1. What feelings did you have about the methods used in the program?

2. What did you like about the information round robin?

3. What did you like about the learning tournament?

4. What didn't you like about the information round robin?

5. What didn't you like about the learning tournament?

Level 2: Learning

Level 2 evaluation deals with learning. What did the participants actually learn in the training session? Kirkpatrick defined learning as the "extent to which participants change attitudes, improve knowledge and/or increase skill as a result of attending the program" (Kirkpatrick, 1994). It is far easier to determine what new knowledge or skills the participants acquired than the ways in which the training changed their opinions, values, and beliefs.

The three most appropriate methods used to evaluate learning are tests, observation, and interviews, with tests being the most frequently used. Given the nature of the new employee orientation program, it would not be advisable to test the new employees. Your goal is to help them become more comfortable with the organization, not scare them away.

Several of the learning activities presented in this workbook lend themselves to a Level 2 evaluation. For example, Learning Activity 10–23: Terminology Tournament enables participants to demonstrate how well they have learned organization and industry jargon and terminology. Learning Activity 10–24: Summary of Learnings gives participants an opportunity to identify the key points they learned in the program.

You also might interview participants a week or two after the program and ask what they learned about the organization. You might combine these Level 2 questions with Level 1 questions that address their reaction to the program.

Level 3: Behavior

The critical question answered by Level 3 is, "How has the training affected the way participants perform on the job?" In the case of a new employee orientation program, the question is, "How has the program helped the new employee assimilate into the organization and his or her work unit?"

Follow-up is an important part of a successful program. The orientation administrator should establish a monitoring system by asking new employees about the effectiveness of the program and soliciting input from managers and supervisors about program improvements and enhancements. Surveys are a fairly efficient and inexpensive way to find out if the participants actually are using what they learned.

As noted in chapter 3, the purpose of an orientation program is to provide information, share ideas, and establish mutual trust from the beginning. Specifically, it should be designed to

1. promote two-way communication

2. reduce anxiety

3. promote a positive employee attitude

4. assimilate the employee into the organization.

Accordingly, the follow-up survey should be designed to measure how well the program met its stated goals and objectives.

A sample follow-up survey (Tool 11–12: 90-Day Follow-up Survey) is presented on page 198 or you may insert the CD and open the file titled *Tool 11–12.pdf.*

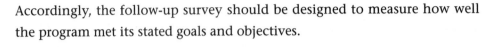

Level 4: Results

Level 4 evaluation assesses the effect of the training on the organization. Ideally, it shows how the training has contributed to accomplishing organizational goals and objectives. This level focuses on business results. If an organization chooses to conduct a Level 4 evaluation, the areas of measurement must be the same as those identified in the needs assessment you conducted with key decision makers prior to developing and implementing the program. In other words, you must determine your critical success factors up-front. Results you wish to measure could include any of the following factors:

- safety record
- turnover rate
- absenteeism
- employee grievances
- employee satisfaction.

Evaluation is a complex issue with many variables that enter into the equation. No matter how hard you try to fine-tune the evaluation process, the reality is that effects can only be estimated, and economic benefits cannot be calculated precisely.

What to Do Next

When the time comes to evaluate your new employee orientation program, here are the steps to take:

- Create an evaluation plan. Decide what, how, and when you want to evaluate the program. Create a plan along with a timeline.

- Develop evaluation form(s). Create your own evaluation form(s) and methods. Get input and feedback from employees who have been with the organization for three to six months.

◆ Gather data. Collect data from participants through a specific assessment piece and/or interviews (one-on-one or in small groups).

◆ Analyze results. Analyze the data collected through various methods. Identify program strengths and areas for improvement. Prepare a report to senior management.

◆ Make revisions as necessary. Based on the results of your evaluation, you will make the appropriate changes to the program such as content, activities, and timeframes.

◆◆◆

Now you are ready to design and develop your program. The next chapter offers a specific, concrete plan for creating a one-day or two-day orientation program that is interactive and personally engaging for the new employee.

Chapter 7

Delivering a Classroom-Based Orientation Program at the Organization Level

* Circumstances calling for a two-day or a one-day program

* Guidelines for choosing the content of two- and one-day sessions

* Sample agenda for a two-day program

* Sample agenda for a one-day program

* Step-by-step program preparation and delivery instructions

The material in this workbook can be adapted easily to a variety of training needs and timeframes. This chapter offers a specific and concrete plan for creating an orientation program geared to all employees, regardless of job level. It provides designs for a two-day program and a one-day program. The designs are flexible enough that you can choose among the activities to supplement your own program design.

Two-Day Program

WHEN TO USE A TWO-DAY PROGRAM

A two-day program is appropriate when

* key people within the organization support a comprehensive program

* the targeted audience is 12 or more

* training facilities for groups are available

* guest facilitators are available.

CHOOSING THE CONTENT

The content should include the following standard topics for a new employee orientation program:

- ◆ Company history and context

- ◆ Compensation and benefits

- ◆ Policies and procedures

- ◆ Employee programs and services.

The subtopics for those categories are listed in chapter 3.

The two-day design is a more comprehensive and, therefore, more effective option than a one-day program. However, the requirements, directives, and resources of your organization will drive the length of your program as well as its content.

STEP-BY-STEP PREPARATION AND DELIVERY

Before the training session:

1. Design the program and schedule the session.

2. Reserve the room and request appropriate seating configuration.

3. Contact guest facilitators and meet with them to prepare them for their sections.

4. Identify new employee program participants and send them an invitation to attend the session.

5. Prepare training materials (handouts, instructions, presentations).

6. Order food and drinks; gather prizes, as needed.

Just prior to the training session:

1. Arrive early at the facility.

2. Set up room (if necessary).

3. Set up and test equipment (that is, flipcharts, projectors).

4. Confirm food and drinks.

5. Place participant materials on tables.

ACTIVITIES AND MATERIALS

Detailed instructions for each learning activity are found in chapter 10, with the tools and handouts that each activity requires. Tools and handouts can be printed directly from the CD that accompanies this workbook. Insert the CD and locate the specific .pdf file for each of the items listed below. You can locate individual slides and PowerPoint presentations on the CD and, if you prefer to use overhead transparencies in your program, those can be printed from the transparency masters on the CD.

The following is a list of the participant handouts and facilitator tools suggested for use in the two-day new employee orientation program:

- ◆ Handout 10–1: Connections Worksheet (page 98; *Handout 10–1.pdf* on the CD)

- ◆ Tool 10–1: Famous Fictional Friends and Families (page 105; *Tool 10–1.pdf* on the CD) or Handout 10–2: At the Movies Participant Instructions (page 108; *Handout 10–2.pdf* on the CD)

- ◆ Tool 10–2: Orientation Bingo! Sample Game Sheet (page 115; *Tool 10–2.pdf* on the CD)

- ◆ Tool 10–3: Orientation Bingo! Sample Key Words and Concepts (page 115; *Tool 10–3.pdf* on the CD)

- ◆ Handout 10–3: Orientation Bingo! Blank Game Sheet (page 116; *Handout 10–3.pdf* on the CD)

- ◆ Handout 10–4: What Do You Know? Worksheet (page 118; *Handout 10–4.pdf* on the CD)

- ◆ Handout 10–5: Our Heritage Worksheet (page 121; *Handout 10–5.pdf* on the CD)

- ◆ Tool 10–4: Sample Organization Chart (page 124; *Tool 10–4.pdf* on the CD)

- ◆ Tool 10–5: Sample Cards (page 125; *Tool 10–5.pdf* on the CD)

- ◆ Handout 10–6: Organizational Scavenger Hunt Search Sheet (page 141; *Handout 10–6.pdf* on the CD)

- ◆ Tool 10–6: Sample Scavenger Hunt Memo (page 142; *Tool 10–6.pdf* on the CD)

◆   Handout 10–7: Policies and Procedures Information Search Worksheet (page 145; *Handout 10–7.pdf* on the CD)

◆   Tool 10–7: Agree/Disagree Cards (page 148; *Tool 10–7.pdf* on the CD)

◆   Handout 10–8: Safety Hazards Worksheet (page 153; *Handout 10–8.pdf* on the CD)

◆   Handout 10–9: Taking the High Road Worksheet (page 159; *Handout 10–9.pdf* on the CD)

◆   Handout 10–10: Whom Do I Contact? Worksheet (page 162; *Handout 10–10.pdf* on the CD)

◆   Handout 10–11: Terminology Tournament Study Sheet (page 165; *Handout 10–11.pdf* on the CD)

◆   Handout 10–12: End-of-Program Questionnaire (page 172 *Handout 10–12.pdf* on the CD).

Two-Day Sample Agenda

TOPIC: THE JOURNEY BEGINS—OPENING ACTIVITIES

9:00 a.m.   *Welcome and Program Objectives*—Lecturette (5 minutes)

Begin your session on time by getting the participants' attention in a fun way (whistle, horn, gong). Display the title slide (slide 7–1). (Numbered thumbnails of slides appear at the end of this chapter.) Introduce yourself (and other facilitators, as appropriate) and welcome the participants. Note the usual housekeeping items such as restroom locations and breaks.

Direct participants' attention to their materials and review the agenda and learning objectives. Explain that they will receive material to add to their binders throughout the program. Show slides 7–2 and 7–3.

9:05   *Icebreaker*—Learning Activity 10–1: Connections (page 96) (20 minutes)

Tell participants that you want to give them an opportunity to get to know each other through several high-energy and fun activities. Introduce Learning Activity

10–1: Connections. After completing and debriefing the activity, award the prizes.

Time-saving variation: Instead of conducting the Connections activity during the formal opening activities, give each participant a Connections worksheet as they enter the room. Direct them to mill around the room and collect signatures before the program actually gets started. (This gives those who arrive early something to do.) Award prizes at the beginning of the opening activities.

9:25   *Introductions*—Learning Activity 10–2: Things We Have in Common (page 99) or Learning Activity 10–3: Representative Items (page 101) (15 minutes)

Explain that participants now will have an opportunity to learn more about each other through another get-acquainted activity. Introduce, conduct, and discuss whichever learning activity you have chosen to use.

Point out that you know how uncomfortable it can be to be "the new kid on the block." Stress that they can minimize their anxiety and increase their comfort level by getting to know people, and that sharing a little of themselves just as they did in this activity can be very helpful in establishing relationships with co-workers.

9:40   *Getting Acquainted*—Learning Activity 10–4: Finding Famous Fictional Friends and Families (page 103) or Learning Activity 10–5: At the Movies (page 106) (30 minutes)

Introduce the next activity by pointing out that each person in the room brings a wealth of knowledge, skills, and experience to the company. Explain that part of being an effective team member is being able to draw on existing talents and apply them to new assignments. Introduce, conduct, and discuss whichever learning activity you have chosen to use.

Tell participants that you hope they are now more comfortable with you and with each other, and that they should draw on what they learned from these get-acquainted activities to help them in their actual job situations.

10:10   Break (15 minutes)

10:25   *Assessing Needs*—Learning Activity 10–6: What Do You Want to Know? (page 109) (15 minutes)

Explain that although you have a plan for this orientation session, you would like to make sure you are on target with what participants hope to gain from the session. Tell them that this next activity will give you some additional insight into their expectations for the session. Introduce, conduct, and discuss Learning Activity 10–6.

10:40   *Team Building*—Learning Activity 10–7: Team Logo (page 111) (30 minutes)

Introduce the next activity by telling participants that one of the best things about working for this organization is being part of a team. Point out that the success and sense of satisfaction they will experience as an employee largely will result from their ability to be a team player. Explain that this learning activity will help them begin to establish a team orientation. Introduce, conduct, and discuss the activity.

TOPIC: INSIDE OUR ORGANIZATION

11:10   *Background and Philosophy*—Learning Activity 10–8: Orientation Bingo! (page 113), Learning Activity 10–9: What Do You Know About Our Organization? (page 117), and Learning Activity 10–10: Our Heritage (page 119) (5 minutes)

Tell participants that throughout the program they will be hearing and learning about key words and phrases that are integral parts of the organization's philosophy. To become familiar with these critical elements, they will participate in an ongoing activity called "Orientation Bingo!" that begins now and will continue throughout the orientation program. Introduce Learning Activity 10–8.

11:15   Introduce Learning Activity 10–9 by explaining that the next step in the orientation program will help them gain a better understanding of the organization and how they fit into the overall picture. (15 minutes)

Mention that you're sure that they come to their new positions with various degrees of knowledge about the organization. Remind them that they may have discovered in the Connections activity at the beginning of the session that some people have friends or relatives who work for the organization and those insiders probably have provided some insight. Others, especially those who are new to the geographical area, may have limited knowledge based only on what they've read or learned about the organization through the interview process. Tell them that you are going to engage them in an activity called "What Do You Know About Our Organization?" to find out what they may or may not already know. Introduce, conduct, and discuss the activity.

11:30   Now tell participants that the next activity is designed to bring them all up to speed not only about what the organization does but also who the organization is. Explain that they will watch a video that provides background about the organization, including its history, products and services, customers, and so forth. Also tell them that they will be given an assignment related to the video, so they will have to be particularly attentive to it. Introduce, conduct, and discuss the activity. (30 minutes)

Noon   Lunch (60 minutes)

1:00 p.m.   *Organizational Structure*—Learning Activity 10–11: Card Sort (page 122) (20 minutes)

Introduce this activity by explaining that every organization has a particular structure, one that can be confusing and overwhelming to a new employee. Tell them that becoming more familiar with the structure of the organization will help put into context the information they receive throughout the rest of the program.

Explain that they will be learning about the organization's structure through an interesting and challenging activity called a "Card Sort." They will be working in teams to figure out for themselves how they think the organization is structured. Emphasize that you do not expect them to know this information already. Introduce, conduct, and discuss the activity.

1:20   *Departments*—Learning Activity 10–12: Information Round Robin (page 129) or Learning Activity 10–13: Press Conference (page 131) (60 minutes)

Tell participants that because they now understand the corporate framework, the next step is to seek more insight into the structural divisions or departments. Explain that they will be participating in an interactive activity to gain more information about the departments and to meet the key people within those areas. Introduce, conduct, and discuss whichever activity you have chosen to use.

2:20   *Products and Services*—Learning Activity 10–14: Poster Sessions (page 133) (50 minutes)

Introduce this activity by telling participants how important it is that they understand the organization's products and/or services. Mention that the more they know about what the organization does, the better they will understand how what they do contributes to the organization's success.

Draw their attention to the posters around the room that depict or represent the organization's products and/or services. Tell the participants that they will be actively involved in learning more about the products and/or services through a series of "poster sessions." Introduce, conduct, and discuss the activity.

3:10   Break (15 minutes)

3:25   *Employees' Perspectives*—Learning Activity 10–15: Panel Discussion (page 136) (30 minutes)

Explain to participants that they are going to have an opportunity to learn about the organization from a different perspective through a structured experience called "Employees' Perspectives." Introduce, conduct, and discuss the learning activity.

3:55   *Building Layout*—Learning Activity 10–16: Organization-al Scavenger Hunt (page 138) (65 minutes)

Tell participants that the next activity is a scavenger hunt designed to increase their familiarity with people, places, and things in the organization. Mention that to make it more interesting and exciting, they will be working in teams to complete the assignment. Introduce, conduct, and discuss the activity.

5:00   Close

TOPIC: HOW WE OPERATE

9:00 a.m.   *Policies and Procedures*—Learning Activity 10–17: Information Search (page 143) (30 minutes)

Introduce this segment by explaining that the organization is committed to helping them become happy, healthy, and productive employees. Tell them that various policies and procedures have been put in place to support them.

Point out that like most other organizations, your organization has developed an employee handbook that provides important information to help ensure the well-being of all employees. Explain that rather than listen to boring presentations highlighting the information in the handbook, they will work in teams to search out critical information in their handbooks. Introduce, conduct, and discuss the activity.

9:30   *Professional Appearance*—Learning Activity 10–18: What Do I Wear? (page 146) (20 minutes)

Tell participants that one of the most troublesome and sometimes confusing aspects in today's work environment is the dress code. Mention that every organization is different—what might be acceptable in one place is totally unacceptable in another environment.

Explain that in this activity they will participate in an activity called "What Do I Wear?" in which they will speculate about what they perceive is appropriate and inappropriate attire and personal grooming in their new work environment. Introduce, conduct, and discuss the activity.

9:50   *Safety Issues*—Learning Activity 10–19: Safety First (page 149) (30 minutes)

Make the transition to this segment by mentioning that every employee is responsible for helping maintain a safe and healthy work environment. Tell them that they are going to find out more about workplace safety issues in this activity. Introduce, conduct, and discuss the activity.

10:20   Break (15 minutes)

10:35   *Core Values*—Learning Activity 10–20: Living Our Core Values (page 154) (40 minutes)

Explain to participants that every organization bases the way it does business on a certain set of values. Sometimes these values are written; sometimes they're simply understood. Mention that their own behavior is guided by certain values that they hold.

Ask for an example of a value and how that particular value affects behavior. Be prepared to offer an example to get them started. For example, if someone values health, that individual makes it a priority to maintain a healthy lifestyle by exercising, eating healthy foods, and getting enough sleep. Likewise, someone who values honesty would not cheat on his or her income tax return. After several people have suggested specific values, show the values slides (slides 7–22 and 7–23) and ask for behavior examples that were not mentioned previously.

Now explain that the learning activity will help them gain a better understanding of how the organization's core values relate to employee behavior. Introduce, conduct, and discuss the activity.

11:15   *Ethics*—Learning Activity 10–21: Taking the High Road (page 156) (45 minutes)

Explain to participants that an organization's ethics policy has a direct bearing on the behavior it expects from its employees. Ask participants for examples of ethical issues they may have heard about recently in the news. Be prepared to cite an example. Tell them that this activity will help them gain a better understanding of the organization's ethics policy. Introduce, conduct, and discuss the activity.

Noon   Lunch (60 minutes)

1:00 p.m.   *Resources*—Learning Activity 10–22: Whom Do I Contact? (page 160) (30 minutes)

Introduce this segment by mentioning to participants that one of their challenges as new employees is to identify where to go or whom to contact when they have a question. To make that process easier, tell them that they now will create their own user-friendly resource list. Introduce, conduct, and discuss the activity.

1:30   *Terminology*—Learning Activity 10–23: Terminology Tournament (page 163) (60 minutes)

Mention that all industries and organizations have their own jargon and terminology that can be very challenging to employees during their first weeks and months on the job. Also mention that a few of them may have been exposed to some of this terminology already and others may be hearing it for the first time. Tell them that you now are going to help them get up to speed with organizational terminology. Introduce, conduct, and discuss the activity.

2:30   Break (15 minutes)

TOPIC: COMING FULL CIRCLE—CLOSING ACTIVITIES

2:45   *Key Points*—Learning Activity 10–24: Summary of Learnings (page 166) (40 minutes) and Learning Activity 10–25: Full Circle (page 167) (15 minutes)

Point out to participants that they have been exposed to a lot of information over the past two days. Tell them you know this orientation experience can be overwhelming, but that you hope they will take some key learning points from the program. Explain that to help them pull together everything that has been covered in the past two days, they will create their own summary of what they have learned. Introduce, conduct, and discuss the activity.

Remind participants that at the very beginning of the program, they identified their questions and concerns through the "What Do You Want to Know?" activity. Tell them that you want to make sure that all their questions and concerns were addressed over the past two days. Explain that they will have an opportunity to make sure you did your job by engaging in an activity called "Full Circle." Introduce, conduct, and discuss the activity.

3:40   *Final Remarks*—Learning Activity 10–26: Reflections (page 168) and Learning Activity 10–27: Group Photo and End-of-Program Questionnaire (page 170) (35 minutes)

Tell the participants that you would like them to think about the most important thing they learned in this orientation program and what has been the most meaningful piece of information or experience for each of them. Mention that the next activity will help focus on the true value of the orientation program. Introduce and conduct the activity.

When the last person has finished sharing his or her reflection, ask participants to remain standing. Tell them that you want each of them to have a remembrance of their shared orientation experience—a group photo. Introduce and conduct the activity. Ask participants to turn in the questionnaires as they leave the room.

4:15   Close

One-Day Program

WHEN TO USE A ONE-DAY PROGRAM

A one-day session is appropriate when

- ◆ key people within the organization will support only an abbreviated program
- ◆ the targeted audience is 12 or more
- ◆ training facilities for groups are available only for one day
- ◆ guest facilitators are available only for one day.

CHOOSING THE CONTENT

The content should include the following standard topics for a new employee orientation program:

- ◆ Company history and context
- ◆ Compensation and benefits
- ◆ Policies and procedures
- ◆ Employee programs and services.

The subtopics for those categories are listed in chapter 3.

STEP-BY-STEP PREPARATION AND DELIVERY

Before the training session:

1. Design the program and schedule the session.

2. Reserve the room and request an appropriate seating configuration.

3. Contact guest facilitators and meet with them to prepare them for their sections.

4. Identify new employee program participants and send them an invitation to attend the session.

5. Prepare training materials (handouts, instructions, presentations).

6. Order food and drinks; gather prizes, as needed.

Just prior to the training session:

1. Arrive early at the facility.

2. Set up room, if necessary.

3. Set up and test equipment (that is, flipcharts, projectors).

4. Confirm food and drinks.

5. Place participant materials on the tables.

ACTIVITIES AND MATERIALS

Detailed instructions for each learning activity are found in chapter 10, with the tools and handouts that each activity requires. Tools and handouts can be printed directly from the CD that accompanies this workbook. Insert the CD and locate the specific .pdf file for each of the items listed below. You can locate individual slides and PowerPoint presentations on the CD and, if you prefer to use overhead transparencies in your program, those can be printed from the transparency masters on the CD.

The following is a list of the facilitator tools and participant handouts suggested for use in the one-day new employee orientation program:

◆ Handout 10–1: Connections Worksheet (page 98; *Handout 10–1.pdf* on the CD)

◆ Tool 10–1: Famous Fictional Friends and Families (page 105; *Tool 10–1.pdf* on the CD) or Handout 10–2: At the Movies Participant Instructions (page 108; *Handout 10–2.pdf* on the CD)

◆ Tool 10–2: Orientation Bingo! Sample Game Sheet (page 115; *Tool 10–2.pdf* on the CD)

◆ Tool 10–3: Orientation Bingo! Sample Key Words and Concepts (page 115; *Tool 10–3.pdf* on the CD)

◆ Handout 10–3: Orientation Bingo! Blank Game Sheet (page 116; *Handout 10–3.pdf* on the CD)

◆ Handout 10–4: What Do You Know? Worksheet (page 118; *Handout 10–4.pdf* on the CD)

◆ Tool 10–4: Sample Organization Chart (page 124; *Tool 10–4.pdf* on the CD)

- Tool 10–5: Sample Cards (page 125; *Tool 10–5.pdf* on the CD)

- Handout 10–6: Organizational Scavenger Hunt Search Sheet (page 141; *Handout 10–6.pdf* on the CD)

- Tool 10–6: Sample Scavenger Hunt Memo (page 142; *Tool 10–6.pdf* on the CD)

- Handout 10–7: Policies and Procedures Information Search Worksheet (page 145; *Handout 10–7.pdf* on the CD)

- Tool 10–7: Agree/Disagree Cards (page 148; *Tool 10–7.pdf* on the CD)

- Handout 10–9: Taking the High Road Worksheet (page 159; *Handout 10–9.pdf* on the CD)

- Handout 10–11: Terminology Tournament Study Sheet (page 165; *Handout 10–11.pdf* on the CD)

- Handout 10–12: End-of-Program Questionnaire (page 172; *Handout 10–12.pdf* on the CD).

One-Day Sample Agenda

TOPIC: THE JOURNEY BEGINS—OPENING ACTIVITIES

8:15 a.m.   *Welcome and Program Objectives*—Lecturette (5 minutes)

Begin your session on time by getting the participants' attention in a fun way (whistle, horn, gong). Display the title slide (slide 7–1). (Numbered thumbnails of slides appear at the end of this chapter.) Introduce yourself (and other facilitators, as appropriate) and welcome the participants. Note the usual housekeeping items such as restroom locations and breaks.

Direct participants' attention to their materials and review the agenda and learning objectives. Explain that they will receive material to add to their binders throughout the program. Show slides 7–2, 7–3, and 7–4.

8:20   *Icebreaker*—Learning Activity 10–1: Connections (page 96) (20 minutes)

Tell participants that you want to give them an opportunity to get to know each other through several high-energy and fun activities. Introduce Learning Activity 10–1: Connections. After completing and debriefing the activity, award the prizes.

Point out that you know how uncomfortable it can be to be "the new kid on the block." Stress that they can minimize their anxiety and increase their comfort level by getting to know people, and that sharing a little of themselves just as they did in this activity can be very helpful in establishing relationships with co-workers.

Time-saving variation: Instead of conducting the Connections activity during the formal opening activities, give each participant a Connections worksheet as they enter the room. Direct them to mill around the room and collect signatures before the program actually gets started. (This gives those who arrive early something to do.) Award prizes at the beginning of the opening activities.

8:40 *Getting Acquainted*—Learning Activity 10–4: Finding Famous Fictional Friends and Families (page 103) (20 minutes)

Introduce the next activity by pointing out that each person in the room brings a wealth of knowledge, skills, and experience to the company. Explain that part of being an effective team member is being able to draw on existing talents and apply them to new assignments. Introduce, conduct, and discuss the activity.

Tell participants that you hope they are now more comfortable with you and with each other, and that they should draw on what they learned from these get-acquainted activities to help them in their actual job situations.

9:00 *Assessing Needs*—Learning Activity 10–6: What Do You Want to Know? (page 109) (15 minutes)

Explain that although you have a plan for this orientation session, you would like to make sure you are on target with what participants hope to gain from the session. Tell them that this next activity will give you some additional insight into their expectations for the session. Introduce, conduct, and discuss Learning Activity 10–6.

TOPIC: INSIDE OUR ORGANIZATION

9:15 *Background and Philosophy*—Learning Activity 10–8: Orientation Bingo! (page 113) and Learning Activity 10–9: What Do You Know About Our Organization? (page 117) (20 minutes)

Tell participants that throughout the program they will be hearing and learning about key words and phrases that are integral parts of the organization's philosophy. To become familiar with these critical elements, they will participate in an ongoing activity called "Orientation Bingo!" that begins now and will continue throughout the orientation program. Introduce Learning Activity 10–8.

Introduce Learning Activity 10–9 by explaining that the next step in the orientation program will help them gain a better understanding of the organization and how they fit into the overall picture.

Mention that you're sure that they come to their new positions with various degrees of knowledge about the organization. Remind them that they may have discovered in the Connections activity at the beginning of the session that some people have friends or relatives who work for the organization and those insiders probably have provided some insight. Others, especially those who are new to the geographical area, may have limited knowledge based only on what they've read or learned about the organization through the interview process. Tell them that you are going to engage them in an activity called "What Do You Know About Our Organization?" to find out what they may or may not already know. Introduce, conduct, and discuss the activity.

Now tell participants that the next activity is designed to bring them all up to speed not only about what the organization does but also who the organization is. Explain that they will watch a video that provides background about the organization, including its history, products and services, customers, and so forth. Also tell them that they will be given an assignment related to the video, so they will have to be particularly attentive to it. Introduce, conduct, and discuss the activity.

9:35   *Organizational Structure*—Learning Activity 10–11: Card Sort (page 122) (20 minutes)

Introduce this activity by explaining that every organization has a particular structure, one that can be confusing and overwhelming to a new employee. Tell them that becoming more familiar with the structure of the organization will help put into context the information they receive throughout the rest of the program.

Explain that they will be learning about the organization's structure through an interesting and challenging activity called a "Card Sort." They will be working in teams to figure out for themselves how they think the organization is structured. Emphasize that you do not expect them to know this information already. Introduce, conduct, and discuss the activity.

9:55   Break (15 minutes)

10:10   *Departments*—Learning Activity 10–12: Information Round Robin (page 129), Learning Activity 10–13: Press Conference (page 131), or Learning Activity 10–14: Poster Sessions (variation) (page 133?) (50 minutes)

Tell participants that because they now understand the corporate framework, the next step is to seek more insight into the structural divisions or departments. Explain that they will be participating in an interactive activity to gain more information about the departments and to meet the key people within those areas. Introduce, conduct, and discuss whichever activity you have chosen to use.

11:00   *Building Layout*—Learning Activity 10–16: Organizational Scavenger Hunt (page 138) (60 minutes)

Tell participants that the next activity is a scavenger hunt designed to increase their familiarity with people, places, and things in the organization. Mention that to make it more interesting and exciting, they will be working in teams to complete the assignment. Introduce, conduct, and discuss the activity.

Noon   Lunch (60 minutes)

TOPIC: HOW WE OPERATE

1:00 p.m.   *Policies and Procedures*—Learning Activity 10–17: Information Search (page 143) (30 minutes)

Introduce this segment by explaining that the organization is committed to helping them become happy, healthy, and productive employees. Tell them that various policies and procedures have been put in place to support them.

Point out that like most other organizations, your organization has developed an employee handbook that provides important information to help ensure the well-being of all employees. Explain that rather than listen to boring presentations highlighting the information in the handbook, they will work in teams to search out critical information in their handbooks. Introduce, conduct, and discuss the activity.

1:30   *Professional Appearance*—Learning Activity 10–18: What Do I Wear? (page 146) (15 minutes)

Tell participants that one of the most troublesome and sometimes confusing aspects in today's work environment is the dress code. Mention that every organization is different—what might be acceptable in one place is totally unacceptable in another environment.

Explain that in this activity they will participate in an activity called "What Do I Wear?" in which they will speculate about what they perceive is appropriate and inappropriate attire and personal grooming in their new work environment. Introduce, conduct, and discuss the activity.

1:45   *Core Values*—Learning Activity 10–20: Living Our Core Values (page 154) (30 minutes)

Explain to participants that every organization bases the way it does business on a certain set of values. Sometimes these values are written; sometimes they're simply understood. Mention that their own behavior is guided by certain values that they hold.

Ask for an example of a value and how that particular value affects behavior. Be prepared to offer an example to get them started. For example, if someone values health, that individual makes it a priority to maintain a healthy lifestyle by exercising, eating healthy foods, and getting enough sleep. Likewise, someone who values honesty would not cheat on his or her income tax return. After several people have suggested specific values, show the values slides (slides 7–22 and 7–23) and ask for behavior examples that were not mentioned previously.

Now explain that the learning activity will help them gain a better understanding of how the organization's core values relate to employee behavior. Introduce, conduct, and discuss the activity.

2:15   Break (15 minutes)

2:30   *Ethics*—Learning Activity 10–21: Taking the High Road (page 156) (30 minutes)

Explain to participants that an organization's ethics policy has a direct bearing on the behavior it expects from its employees. Ask participants for examples of ethical issues they may have heard about recently in the news. Be prepared to cite an example. Tell them that this activity will help them gain a better understanding of the organization's ethics policy. Introduce, conduct, and discuss the activity.

3:00   *Terminology*—Learning Activity 10–23: Terminology Tournament (page 163) (45 minutes)

Mention that all industries and organizations have their own jargon and terminology that can be very challenging to employees during their first weeks and months on the job. Also mention that a few of them may have been exposed to some of this terminology already and others may be hearing it for the first time. Tell them that you now are going to help them get up to speed with organizational terminology. Introduce, conduct, and discuss the activity.

TOPIC: COMING FULL CIRCLE—CLOSING ACTIVITIES

3:45   *Key Points*—Learning Activity 10–24: Summary of Learnings (page 166) and Learning Activity 10–25: Full Circle (page 167) (30 minutes)

Point out to participants that they have been exposed to a lot of information during the day. Tell them you know this orientation experience can be overwhelming, but that you hope they will take some key learning points from the program. Explain that to help them pull together everything that has been covered in the orientation, they will create their own summary of what they've learned. Introduce, conduct, and discuss the activity.

Remind participants that at the very beginning of the program, they identified their questions and concerns through the "What Do You Want to Know?" activity. Tell them that you want to make sure that all their questions and concerns were addressed. Explain that they will have an opportunity to make sure you did your job by engaging in an activity called "Full Circle." Introduce, conduct, and discuss the activity.

4:15   *Final Remarks*—Learning Activity 10–26: Reflections (page 168) and Learning Activity 10–27: Group Photo and End-of-Session Questionnaire (page 170) (30 minutes)

Tell the participants that you would like them to think about the most important thing they learned in this orientation program and what has been the most meaningful piece of information or experience for each of them.

Mention that the next activity will help focus on the true value of the orientation program. Introduce and conduct the activity.

When the last person has finished sharing his or her reflection, ask participants to remain standing. Tell them that you want each of them to have a remembrance of their shared orientation experience—a group photo. Introduce and conduct the activity. Ask participants to turn in the questionnaires as they leave the room.

4:45   Close

What to Do Next

- ◆ Determine the length of your program.

- ◆ Prepare you own outline and agenda.

- ◆ Gather and prepare participant and facilitator materials for your program.

◆◆◆

In addition to an organization-level orientation, it's important that each department conducts a more targeted orientation that helps the new employee assimilate into the actual work environment. The next chapter presents a highly individualized and customized departmental orientation program.

Slide 7–1

Welcome to

[Name of Organization]

New Employee Orientation Program

Slide 7–2

Benefits of Attending This Program

You will...

- become more knowledgeable about our organization and its rich history
- meet new colleagues and team members
- be introduced to key people within our organization

Slide 7–3

Benefits of Attending This Program

You will...

- learn about the policies and procedures that determine how we operate
- identify where to go for information or answers to questions
- become more familiar with organization and industry terminology

Slide 7–4

Benefits of Attending This Program

You will...

- gain information about key areas of the organization
- identify the tangible and intangible benefits of working here
- develop a sense of being a part of the team
- have fun!

Slide 7–5

Things We Have in Common

- List things you all have in common.
- Identify as many similarities as possible.
- Seek interesting and unusual items.

Slide 7–6

Representative Items

- Select an item that represents who you are.
- Take turns showing items and explain why that item represents you.

Slide 7–7

What Do You Know About Our Organization?

1. Our organization has ____ locations in ____ states and ____ countries.

Slide 7–8

What Do You Know About Our Organization?

2. We employ approximately ____ workers worldwide.

Slide 7–9

What Do You Know About Our Organization?

3. We have been in business ____ years.

Slide 7–10

What Do You Know About Our Organization?

4. Our corporate colors are _____ .

Slide 7–11

What Do You Know About Our Organization?

5. The CEO of our organization is _____ .

Slide 7–12

What Do You Know About Our Organization?

6. Our company Website is_____ .

Slide 7–13

What Do You Know About Our Organization?

7. The name of our company's newsletter is _____ .

Slide 7–14

What Do You Know About Our Organization?

8. Our best-known (or best-selling) product is _____ .

Slide 7–15

What Do You Know About Our Organization?

9. Our parent company is _____ .

Slide 7–16

What Do You Know About Our Organization?

10. Our biggest competitor is _____ .

Slide 7–17

What Is Appropriate? (Agree/Disagree)

Sandals or open-toed shoes

Slide 7–18

What Is Appropriate? (Agree/Disagree)

Short skirts

Slide 7–19

What Is Appropriate?
(Agree/Disagree)

Denim pants or skirts

Slide 7–20

What Is Appropriate?
(Agree/Disagree)

Body piercing

Slide 7–21

What Is Appropriate?
(Agree/Disagree)

Tank tops

Slide 7–22

Values

- Honesty and Integrity
- Loyalty and Trust
- Promotion and Growth
- Mental and Physical Health

Slide 7–23

Values

- Freedom and Independence
- Reward and Recognition
- Relationships
- Power and Influence

Slide 7–24

Reflections

What did you most enjoy about your
orientation experience?

Conducting a Departmental Orientation

- Purpose and objectives of a departmental orientation program

- Preparations for a new worker's arrival in the department

- Supervisor's responsibilities throughout the employee's first week on the job

The manager or supervisor plays a key role in the departmental orientation process. He or she usually is the first one to have contact with the new employee and so becomes the most influential person in developing the new employee's attitudes and impressions. The supervisor is responsible for giving the new employee the tools and resources to be successful in the new position.

This chapter presents a highly individualized and customized departmental orientation plan. In addition to the timelines, topics, and activities, the chapter addresses strategies for assimilating the new employee into the actual work environment and into the organization's culture.

Goals of the Departmental Orientation Process

Orienting the new employee is intended

- to develop good communications with the new employee from the start

- to introduce the new employee to departmental goals, policies and procedures, customs, and traditions

- to convey responsibilities and expectations clearly

- to provide the new employee with information that will ease the transition into his or her workplace.

Preparation for the Employee's Arrival

Take the following actions to prepare for a new worker in the department:

- ◆ **Inform the staff** that a new employee will be joining the department. Tell them when the employee will arrive, what he or she will be doing, and where he or she will be located; and share some specific information, such as previous job, background, qualifications. Look at Tool 11–2: Sample Memo to the New Employee's Co-workers (page 178, or *Tool 11–2.pdf* on the CD).

- ◆ **Send pertinent materials and information** to the new employee. Tool 11–4: Materials to Send Before the New Employee's First Day (page 182, or *Tool 11–4.pdf* on the CD) is a checklist of likely materials.

- ◆ **Prepare the employee's work area.** Make sure the following items are available: supplies, equipment, manuals, forms, directories, and a telephone. See Tool 11–5: New Employee's Work Area Preparation Checklist (page 184, or *Tool 11–5.pdf* on the CD) for guidance.

- ◆ **Select a department member to be the newcomer's "buddy."** This buddy's responsibilities will be to show the new worker around the department, make introductions, answer questions, and generally help make him or her feel welcome and included in the group. The person selected should have many of the same qualities as a designated trainer. In fact, the same person could fill both roles. The advantage of using two different people is that the new employee will be exposed to more people and placed in different relationships and situations.

- ◆ **Review the information to be covered with the employee on the first day.** Several tools are presented to help you with this: Tool 11–6: Activities for the New Employee's First Day (page 186, or *Tool 11–6.pdf* on the CD), Tool 11–7: Information to Communicate During the Employee's First Day (page 188, or *Tool 11–7.pdf* on the CD), and Tool 11–8: Suggested First-Day Work-Related Assignments (page 190, or *Tool 11–8.pdf* on the CD).

On the Employee's First Day

In most companies, the employee will report first to the human resources department to receive benefits information, sign the necessary employment processing forms, and be given an employee handbook or equivalent outlining the company's policies and procedures.

Approximately midmorning, the employee will leave the human resources department to report to his or her work site. The supervisor should greet the new employee personally and set aside adequate time to introduce him or her to the work environment.

First-day orientation is not something a supervisor should delegate. It's too important. This initial interaction establishes lines of communication between the supervisor and the new worker. The supervisor's responsibility is to set the tone and create an environment that helps reduce the employee's anxiety. The relationship between these two people is critical to the employee's success on the job.

The supervisor should begin by getting acquainted with the employee, relating on a personal level, asking questions about the family and about the employee's feelings in starting a new job. The next step is to review the job duties and responsibilities; performance expectations and standards; and company policies, such as sick leave, vacations, work hours, pay, dress code, overtime, smoking policy, and customs. In addition, the employee should receive a departmental information packet containing an organizational chart, department and organization telephone directory, manuals, safety rules, health regulations, and such other helpful information as company brochures, the employee newsletter, the annual report, and a list of resource people. To ensure uniformity and consistency, the supervisor should prepare a checklist of topics to be addressed during the orientation period. Be sure to give a copy to the new employee so he or she will know what to expect. Because the organization orientation will cover personnel policies and practices as well as a more global view of the company as a whole, this particular checklist should address items peculiar to the department and the person's actual job.

An important and often overlooked area is an explanation of the unwritten practices within the department itself—the social norms, such as kitchen clean-up, coffee pot care, birthday rituals, parties, and other accepted behavior peculiar to that department. Failure to do so can result in a real disaster. One new employee helped herself to the last cup of coffee. Because it was the end of the day, she washed both the pot and cup and put them back in place. The next morning when she entered the coffee area, one of her co-workers screamed, "Did you drink the last cup of coffee yesterday?" Without waiting for an answer, she continued, "Around here, the person who empties the pot is responsible for making a fresh one. Don't let it happen again." The new employee was hurt and embarrassed and went out of her way to avoid any further contact with that co-worker. Such a humiliating experience could have been avoided if the supervisor had just taken a minute to explain the department's practice. Such unwritten practices should be communicated to everyone new to the department—not just new hires. People who have been with the organization for a period of time and are transferred to a new department often are overlooked. Remember that this is a totally new environment for the transferee, too.

With preliminaries out of the way, the supervisor should begin acclimating the newcomer to the work unit itself by giving him or her a few minutes to settle into his or her work space. Then the supervisor should tour the work area with the new employee, introducing co-workers and pointing out the locations of restrooms, supply areas, lunch facilities, the photocopy and fax machines, bulletin boards, the mail room, and adjacent departments. At this point, it would be appropriate to introduce the new employee to the chosen buddy or mentor and allow time for the two to get acquainted. This get-acquainted process could be facilitated by having the co-worker show the new employee how to operate the telephone system, the photocopier, and other equipment; how to order supplies; and other operational details. The co-worker also should accompany the newcomer to lunch, taking care to introduce him or her to others in the organization.

At the end of the day, the supervisor should meet once again with the new hire to answer any questions, review important information, give encouragement, and reinforce how pleased everyone in the department is to have the new worker on the team.

On the Employee's Second Day

On the second day, the on-the-job training process should begin with the designated trainer greeting the new employee first thing in the morning. As discussed in other chapters, the on-the-job training should be structured and designed to get the employee working comfortably on his or her own as quickly as possible. The employee's mentor should remain in the picture, arranging to go on breaks and lunches together and offering support.

During the Employee's First Week

Take a look at Tool 11–9: Activities for the New Employee's First Week (page 192, or *Tool 11–9.pdf* on the CD). At the end of the first week, the manager should meet with the employee once again to check on his or her progress; answer questions; and provide additional information, such as department goals and objectives, the performance planning and evaluation process, and career development opportunities. At this point, the manager also may want to review the company's mission statement and goals and explain how the department and the individual fit into the total organization. On the other hand, a discussion of "the big picture" might be more relevant and meaningful if delayed until after the employee's initial adjustment period.

What to Do Next

- ◆ Refer to chapter 11 and the brief descriptions of the helpful tools and checklists.

- ◆ Adapt checklists to reflect your specific situation.

◆◆◆

The following chapter addresses the special considerations of nontraditional employment arrangements, including contract, temporary, and telecommuting employees.

Delivering Distance Orientation

- Suggestions for creating a new employee orientation program for workers at remote sites

- Designs for supervisor-facilitated small-group and one-on-one sessions

- Discussion of computer-based and self-directed program delivery

Today's workplace offers a variety of employment options, including a growing number of contract and temporary employees and telecommuters. These non-traditional employment arrangements require a different orientation approach.

Special Considerations

Sometimes it just is not cost-effective or practical to bring employees to a central location for an orientation session. People often are spread out among remote sites and locations, and bringing them to the corporate headquarters can be very costly. Some organizations, particularly small to mid-size ones, seldom hire new employees so opportunities for timely group sessions are rare. Although such situations may prevent you from conducting traditional group orientations, you still may develop and administer a structured new employee orientation program.

This chapter also presents strategies for designing an orientation program that serves employees who may spend weeks or months in training before they are placed in specific departments or branches. Such circumstances may create a sense of isolation and disconnection, but the lack of corporate identity can be greatly minimized through an orientation program adapted to meet those special situations.

Content

No matter what the format or venue, the orientation content does not change. New employees at remote sites need the same information as do those located at corporate headquarters. Therefore, start designing a distance new employee orientation program by selecting the content you want to present. Refer to chapter 3, "Designing an Interactive Program," for content ideas.

Delivery Methods

When you are certain which information you want to include, the next step is to determine the method or methods you are going to use to deliver it. You have several options, depending on the resources and capabilities available to you and, more importantly, available to the new employee. The delivery methods fall into three broad categories:

1. manager- or supervisor-facilitated delivery

2. technology- and computer-based delivery

3. self-directed or self-study delivery.

You may choose one of the delivery methods or create any combination. Once again, your organization's unique circumstances and its management philosophy will drive the decisions.

MANAGER- OR SUPERVISOR-FACILITATED DELIVERY

One fairly low-cost and low-tech delivery method is to develop a packaged program to be facilitated by the new employee's manager or supervisor. The program developer prepares materials, a leader's guide, and perhaps a video, and sends the package to each site. Many of the learning activities described in chapter 10 can be adapted for use with a smaller group or even in one-on-one orientations. Similarly, the tools in chapter 11 can be useful.

Design for a Small-Group Session

A small group is any number of people between three and 12. When designing a supervisor- or manager-facilitated program, be sensitive to the realities of the everyday business environment. First, managers and supervisors have other responsibilities and do not have a lot of time to prepare for and deliver a program. If they view this additional responsibility as an intrusion or inconvenience, they may not give it the attention it deserves or, worse, may decide to eliminate it altogether. Second, because the new employees are already on the job and engaged in their specific job-related tasks and responsibilities, it may be difficult to pull them off the job for large blocks of time.

The solution to these potential problems is to scale down or chunk the program into manageable segments conducted over a period of weeks and months. The key is to make the process user-friendly. With that in mind, what follows is a suggested design for a supervisor-facilitated program broken down into one-hour segments.

Session 1   *Objectives*—Lecturette

Getting Acquainted—Learning Activity 10–3: Representative Items (page 101)

Assessing Needs—Learning Activity 10–6: What Do You Want to Know? (page 109)

Background and Philosophy—Learning Activity 10–9: What Do You Know About Our Organization? (page 117) and Learning Activity 10–10: Our Heritage (page 119)

Session 2   *Organizational Structure*—Learning Activity 10–11: Card Sort (page 122)

Products and Services—Learning Activity 10–14: Poster Sessions (variation) (page 133)

Session 3   *Policies and Procedures*—Learning Activity 10–17: Information Search (page 143)

Professional Appearance—Learning Activity 10–18: What Do I Wear? (page 146)

Session 4   *Core Values*—Learning Activity 10–20: Living Our Core Values (page 154)

Ethics—Learning Activity 10–21: Taking the High Road (page 156)

Session 5   *Resources*—Learning Activity 10–22: Whom Do I Contact? (page 160)

Terminology—Learning Activity 10–23: Terminology Tournament (page 163)

Key Points—Learning Activity 10–24: Summary of Learnings (page 166)

Design for a One-on-One Session

Even a one-on-one session can be interactive and fun. In most one-on-one sessions, the supervisor sits down with the employee and reviews information. The problem with that approach is that it easily can become an information dump. The communication is primarily one-way, with the supervisor talking *at* the employee and then asking, "Do you understand? Do you have any questions?" Both questions result in "yes" or "no" answers and do little to promote two-way communication between the supervisor and employee.

A more interesting and interactive approach is to give information to the new employee to read on his or her own. Appropriate material would be the employee handbook, brochures describing products and services, and other critical pieces of information that the employee needs to know. It's best to chunk the information and then set up individual meetings to discuss the assigned material. During these one-on-one discussion sessions, the supervisor can "test" the employee's knowledge or understanding of the material by asking open-ended questions. For example, the supervisor might ask, "What is our organization's mission statement and what do you think it means?" The supervisor also can use some of the activities he or she would use in a group session. Here is a list of some activities the new employee could do individually:

- ◆ Learning Activity 10–10: Our Heritage (page 119)

- ◆ Learning Activity 10–11: Organizational Structure Card Sort (page 122)

- ◆ Learning Activity 10–17: Policies and Procedures Information Search (page 143)

- ◆ Learning Activity 10–20: Living Our Core Values (page 154)

- ◆ Learning Activity 10–21: Taking the High Road (page 156)

- ◆ Learning Activity 10–22: Whom Do I Contact? (page 160).

TECHNOLOGY- AND COMPUTER-BASED DELIVERY

The term *computer-based* is used widely to include delivery via CD-ROM, intranet, or Internet. Organizations with video conferencing or teleconferencing capabilities may choose one of those options to deliver their new employee orientation programs. Before you get excited about these state-of-the-art approaches, carefully consider the costs involved with their development and the resources necessary to implement them. Make sure that the new employees have access to a computer with the appropriate bandwidth.

Another consideration of any computer-based approach is the issue of updates. You need a program administrator to monitor the program and make sure the information is up-to-date and accurate. It's also important to select a delivery platform that lends itself to easy and cost-effective updates. Keep in mind, however, that all of these technology-based delivery methods tend to be impersonal and thus defeat the purpose of making the new employee feel welcome and a part of the team.

SELF-DIRECTED OR SELF-STUDY DELIVERY

A self-directed program involves a combination of self-study activities to be completed by the employee on the job and frequent one-on-one meetings with the supervisor. Depending on the available resources, this approach could involve a combination of computer-based and supervisor-facilitated activities. Once again, you can adapt many of the learning activities described in chapter 10. In fact, activities listed above in the "Design for a One-on-One Session" section can be adapted to computer-based delivery methods. For more information on turning classroom-based group activities into technology-based activities, refer to Hank Payne's chapter, "How to Adapt On-Site Exercises to Distance Learning Exercises: Practical Applications," in Mantyla (1999).

What to Do Next

- ◆   Develop a plan for a manager-facilitated small-group session.

- ◆   Develop a plan for a one-on-one session.

- ◆   Develop a plan for a self-directed or self-study program.

◆ ◆ ◆

The next chapter includes the detailed learning activities identified in chapter 7. These highly interactive activities are the key to an effective orientation program that will help make the first few days and weeks of an employee's new job an enjoyable and rewarding experience.

Learning Activities

What's in This Chapter?

- Twenty-seven learning activities
- Nineteen tools and handouts to accompany the activities

This chapter presents all the learning activities identified in the training designs found in chapters 7, 8, and 9. Each learning activity description includes the following information:

- **Objective(s).** The objective identifies how participation in the activity will help the participants. Most objectives address cognitive learning (for example, learning about the history of the organization). Some objectives are targeted toward behavior (for example, locating a specific item). Finally, a few learning activities have affective objectives (for example, heightening the new employee's awareness and sensitivity about appropriate dress).

- **Materials.** Included in the list is everything the trainer needs for a specific activity. The master copy of a required handout or helpful tool appears at the end of the activity or can be printed from the appropriate .pdf file on the accompanying CD. For some activities, handouts included in the text and on the CD will have to be adapted to fit the organization. Program facilitators or guest presenters must provide handouts that are very specific to the organization (for example, mission statement, employee handbook, product information).

- **Time.** This defines the total amount of time needed to complete the activity, including its introduction, the actual experience, and its question-based discussion following the experience.

◆ **Preparation.** This section offers brief instructions on what the facilitator needs to do to prepare for the activity. Possible activities include copying handouts, preparing flipchart pages, making slides, or gathering materials.

◆ **Instructions.** For each learning activity, I have provided step-by-step instructions for introducing and conducting the activity. Although not scripted, these instructions address what the facilitator should say and do to make the activity a success. The emphasis is on facilitation techniques.

◆ **Appropriate Variations.** Some activities include variations. You may choose to use the modified approach, based on time constraints, the size of the group, or your own creativity.

◆ **Discussion Questions for Debriefing.** The success of any activity depends on the discussion that follows it. In fact, this debriefing or processing stage is where the real learning takes place. The discussion questions included with each learning activity are only suggestions. You may use them as written, modify as appropriate to your situation, or add your own questions.

Each of the learning activities is a self-contained design. Accordingly, each can be used in several ways and with programs of various lengths and various group sizes. Some activities can even be modified for use in one-on-one orientation sessions as described in chapters 8 and 9.

Using the Accompanying CD

You will find the handouts and tools included in this chapter and in chapter 11 on the CD that accompanies this workbook. To access these files, insert the CD and click on the following file names:

◆ *Tool [number].pdf*

◆ *Handout [number].pdf*

To print out the materials for your orientation session, follow these simple steps. Insert the CD and click on the appropriate .pdf file name to open it in Adobe Acrobat software. Print out the pages of the document(s) you need.

In this chapter, the slides referred to in each of the learning activities are numbered according to the order in which they appear in chapter 7. You can access individual slides by opening the PowerPoint presentation *New Employee.ppt.*

For additional instructions on using the CD, see the appendix, "Using the Compact Disc," at the end of the workbook.

Learning Activity 10–1: Connections

OBJECTIVE

The objective of this activity is to help participants get to know each other in an enjoyable and nonthreatening way.

MATERIALS

The materials needed for this activity are

- ◆ Handout 10–1: Connections Worksheet

- ◆ Your choice of prizes.

TIME

- ◆ 20 minutes

PREPARATION

1. Prior to the session, make one copy of the handout for each participant. If there are fewer than 20 participants, adjust the number of items on the handout accordingly.

2. Purchase three to five prizes.

INSTRUCTIONS

1. Distribute Handout 10–1. Tell participants that when you give a signal, you want them to move around the room and find fellow participants who meet the 20 criteria listed on the sheet. People will sign their names on the lines that correspond to their criterion, but a person may sign another person's sheet only one time. Tell them they have eight minutes to complete their sheets. As soon as their sheets are filled, they are to hand them in to you.

2. At the end of the designated period, call time and award prizes to the first few people who have their sheets completed or to those who have gotten the most signatures. (You determine how many receive prizes.)

3. Select four or five interesting criteria on the list and ask participants to hold up their hands if they met a particular criterion.

DISCUSSION QUESTIONS FOR DEBRIEFING

Discuss the value of the activity by asking the following questions:

1. What did you experience while you were getting signatures?

2. What did you learn from the activity?

3. How can what you learned help you in your job?

Handout 10–1

Connections Worksheet

Instructions: Read each item below and find someone in this group to whom it applies. Ask that person to sign his or her name on the adjacent line. A person may sign your sheet only one time.

Find someone who . . .

1. has the same first initial as you have.   _____

2. has worked for more than two other companies.   _____

3. grew up in the same town as you did.   _____

4. knows someone who works for the company.   _____

5. lives more than 45 minutes from work.   _____

6. has been told he or she is a good cook.   _____

7. is taking courses or working on a degree.   _____

8. has more than two pets.   _____

9. has lived in more than two states.   _____

10. sleeps less than seven hours a night.   _____

11. enjoys the same type of music as you do.   _____

12. has more than three children.   _____

13. has worked for one of our competitors.   _____

14. was born in the same month as you were.   _____

15. has done volunteer work.   _____

16. is active in a civic or professional organization.   _____

17. plays a musical instrument.   _____

18. is working on a graduate or undergraduate degree. _____

19. has the same number of siblings as you have.   _____

20. enjoys playing team sports.   _____

Learning Activity 10–2:
Things We Have in Common

OBJECTIVES

The objectives of this activity are to help participants

◆ get to know each other

◆ become more comfortable in the work environment.

MATERIALS

The materials needed for this activity are

◆ paper and pen or pencil for each group

◆ prizes, if desired

◆ PowerPoint slide or transparency 7–5.

TIME

◆ 15 minutes

INSTRUCTIONS

1. Use this activity for a group of four or more people. If you have a group of more than six people, create small groups of no more than five people.

2. Ask people in each group to come up with a list of things they all have in common (other than working for the same company). Explain that each group will need an official scribe to record the characteristics.

    ◆ Examples of characteristics: They all are parents, are married, live in houses, take a vacation every year, and so forth.

    ◆ The objective is to come up with as many similarities as possible within a limited amount of time. Give them three or four minutes.

3. Call time after three or four minutes. If you have more than one group, survey the room for the group that has the most items on its list. Ask the winning (or only) group to share its list. You may want

to give prizes to the group with the most items or the most interesting or unusual item.

DISCUSSION QUESTIONS FOR DEBRIEFING

Discuss the activity by asking the following questions:

1. What did you experience during the activity?

2. What did you learn?

3. What was the value of the activity?

You may want to point out that identifying things they have in common with their new co-workers can be helpful in building relationships.

Learning Activity 10–3: Representative Items

OBJECTIVE

The objective of this activity is to help participants introduce themselves in a fun and nonthreatening way.

MATERIALS

The materials needed for this activity are

- ◆ PowerPoint slide or transparency 7–6

- ◆ one small toy for each participant (variation).

TIME

- ◆ 10–15 minutes

INSTRUCTIONS

1. Ask participants to select an item from their briefcases, purses, pockets, or wallets that they believe represents who they are or represents an important aspect of their lives.

2. After everyone has selected an item, have the participants take turns showing their items and explaining why that item represents them.

VARIATION

1. Instead of having participants choose an item, randomly give each one a toy that he or she will use to reveal something about himself or herself. If the group is small, you can place all the toys on a table and ask participants to select one.

2. Ask participants to spend a minute observing their toys and getting acquainted with them.

3. Next, explain that you want them to think about how the toy they selected represents them as a new employee.

4. Ask for a volunteer to share his or her insight with the rest of the group. (If the group is large, you may want to create several small groups.) Continue soliciting volunteers until everyone has had an opportunity to participate.

5. Discuss the activity by asking how they felt about using a toy to represent themselves. What did they learn about themselves? What did they learn about each other?

 ## *DISCUSSION QUESTIONS FOR DEBRIEFING*

Discuss this activity by asking the following questions of the entire group:

1. How did you feel about sharing your representative item with the others?

2. What did you learn about yourself and others?

3. What is the value of this activity?

Learning Activity 10–4: Finding Famous Fictional Friends and Families

OBJECTIVE

The objective of this activity is to help participants get to know each other in a fun and nonthreatening way.

MATERIALS

The materials needed for this activity are

- ◆ Tool 10–1: Famous Fictional Friends and Families

- ◆ index cards (equal to the number of participants)

- ◆ a whistle

- ◆ flipchart pages

- ◆ pen or pencil for each participant.

TIME

- ◆ 30 minutes

PREPARATION

1. Prior to the session, create famous fictional family member or friends index cards. To prepare, choose the same number of fictional family members or friends as there are participants. See Tool 10–1 for fictional individuals and groups.

2. Write the name of one fictional character on a each index card.

3. Shuffle the cards.

4. Prepare flipchart pages with the questions noted in step 6 of the Instructions.

INSTRUCTIONS

1. Explain that this activity is an opportunity to get to know the people in the room from both a professional and a personal perspective.

2. Distribute one index card to each participant.

3. Explain that each person's job is to find the other members of his or her famous group. Tell them how many members should be in each group. (There may be some variations; therefore, you could say that some groups may have four members and some may have five.)

4. Tell them that when you blow your whistle (or make some other audible signal), they are to get up and move around the room, trying to find the other members of their groups. Don't give participants any extra information. Tell them to ask their colleagues for help if they don't know the character they've been assigned. Give them three or four minutes to form their groups. Tell them to find a spot in the room to congregate.

5. At the end of the designated time period (or when all groups have been formed), signal to get the groups' attention.

6. Refer them to the flipchart pages listing the following questions:

   ◆ What is the position you have been hired for?

   ◆ What is your reason for joining the company?

   ◆ What is one thing you would like others to know about you?

7. Tell them to spend the next six to eight minutes sharing the answers to the above questions with the other members of their group.

8. At the end of that discussion period, call time and ask for volunteers to share the most interesting things they learned about someone in their group.

DISCUSSION QUESTIONS FOR DEBRIEFING

Discuss the activity by asking the following questions:

1. How did you feel at the beginning of the activity as you were searching for your group?

2. How is that experience similar to what you may experience during your first few days on the job?

3. How did you go about finding your group?

4. What did you learn from this activity?

5. How can this experience help you as you begin your new job?

Tool 10–1

Famous Fictional Friends and Families

- ◆ Peter Pan, Wendy, Tinkerbell, Captain Hook, Crocodile

- ◆ Robin Hood, Maid Marian, Friar Tuck, the Sheriff of Nottingham, Little John

- ◆ Superman, Clark Kent, Lois Lane, Jimmy Olsen, Perry White

- ◆ Hawkeye, Trapper John, Hot Lips, Radar, Klinger

- ◆ Han Solo, Princess Leia, Darth Vadar, R2D2, Luke Skywalker

- ◆ Cowardly Lion, Tin Man, Dorothy, Toto, Scarecrow

- ◆ Alice, Cheshire Cat, Queen of Hearts, Mad Hatter, White Rabbit

- ◆ Mickey Mouse, Minnie Mouse, Pluto, Donald Duck, Goofy

- ◆ Charlie Brown, Linus, Lucy, Snoopy, Odie

- ◆ Winnie the Pooh, Tigger, Piglet, Eeyore, Roo

Learning Activity 10–5: At the Movies

OBJECTIVE

The objective of this activity is to help participants get acquainted at the beginning of the orientation session.

MATERIALS

For this activity, you need

- Handout 10–2: At the Movies Participant Instructions

- a selection of vintage or contemporary movie posters—ones that attendees are likely to have seen.

TIME

- 30–45 minutes

PREPARATION

1. Make one copy of the handout for each participant.

2. Hang or display movie posters on the walls or on easels around the room.

INSTRUCTIONS

1. Distribute Handout 10–2 to each participant.

2. Tell participants that they are to look around the room at the movie posters and select their three favorite films. Explain that there will be three rounds of activity. During Round #1, participants are to go to the area designated for their first movie choice; in Round #2, the area designated for their second choice; and in Round #3, the area designated for their third choice.

3. When the groups have formed for each round, ask participants to discuss the questions or topics that appear on their instruction sheet for that round.

   Round #1   ◆   Introduce yourself to your group members by stating your name, where you live, and your position and responsibilities.

        ◆   Explain briefly why you selected this particular movie as your favorite.

Round #2   ◆   Identify something you have in common with the other members in your group. Possible topics might include hobbies, sports activities, family, pets, or job.

Round #3   ◆   What is the greatest strength you bring (or contribution you can make) to this organization?

4. After the first two rounds, the facilitator will process the activity by selecting participants at random to respond to the following questions:

Round #1   ◆   Who in your group traveled the farthest?
            ◆   Why did you like this movie?

Round #2   ◆   What did you find you have in common?

5. Use the following time allowances:

- eight minutes for each group discussion

- three minutes for movement between rounds

- five minutes after each round for processing.

VARIATION

Instead of using movies, you may choose other topics, such as

- sport or leisure activities you enjoy

- famous people you would like to meet

- country you would like to visit

- animal you would like to have as a pet.

DISCUSSION QUESTIONS FOR DEBRIEFING

Discuss the activity by asking the following questions:

1. What did you experience during the activity?

2. What was the most interesting thing you learned about someone else?

3. What was the value of this activity?

4. How can your experience in this activity benefit you as you begin your new job?

Handout 10–2
At the Movies Participant Instructions

1. Look around the room at the movie posters and select your three favorite movies. This activity will consist of three rounds of groupings or gatherings. During Round #1, you are to go to the area designated for your first movie choice; Round #2, your second choice; Round #3, your third choice.

2. There should be no more than seven people in a group; therefore, if the group you choose is full, move to your next choice.

3. When your groups are formed, follow these instructions:

    Round #1   ◆ Introduce yourself to your group members by stating your name, where you live, and your position and responsibilities.

                    ◆ Explain briefly why you selected this particular movie as your favorite.

    Round #2   ◆ Identify something you have in common with the other members in your group. Possible topics might include hobbies, sports activities, family, pets, or job.

    Round #3   ◆ What is the greatest strength you bring (or contribution you can make) to this organization?

4. Each round will be eight minutes long. Your facilitator will give a signal when it's time to move to the next group.

Learning Activity 10–6:
What Do You Want to Know?

OBJECTIVE

The objective of this activity is to help participants focus on their specific orientation needs.

MATERIALS

The materials needed for this activity are

- pad of Post-it notes for each participant

- flipchart pages

- markers

- masking tape.

TIME

- 15 minutes

PREPARATION

1. Prepare flipchart pages by writing on them the general topics that will be addressed in the session, one topic to a page. For example, one page may be labeled "Benefits," another "Company History," others "Organization Structure/Departments," "Products/Services," and so forth. Label one page "Parking Lot."

2. Tape the flipchart pages to the wall.

3. Distribute a pad of Post-it notes to each participant.

INSTRUCTIONS

1. Explain that although you have a plan for the program, you want to make sure you are on target with what attendees want to get out of the program.

2. Point out that you have posted flipchart pages on the wall with the general topics to be covered in the program. Using the Post-it notes you distributed earlier, they are to write down questions they have

about the topics. They have five minutes to write their questions, and they may write as many questions as they want—one per Post-it note.

3. At the end of five minutes, ask participants to get up and stick their questions on the appropriate topic pages.

4. After all questions have been posted, quickly group similar questions, and briefly summarize or point out the most common questions. If participants have posted questions that will not (or cannot) be addressed in this session, move them to the "Parking Lot" page and explain why the question will not be addressed. Also, be sure to tell them where, when, or how they will be able to get the answers to those "parked" questions or concerns.

VARIATIONS

1. Depending on time constraints and/or the size of the group, you may want to limit the number of questions generated. If that is the case, form small groups of four or five people.

2. Ask each group to develop a list of what its members want to know. You may limit how many items the groups generate—three or four is a workable number.

3. Tell groups to select someone to record the group's items and a spokesperson. Give them a time limit of five or six minutes to complete their questions.

4. At the end of the time period, ask for a volunteer to begin the reporting process. Be sure to limit each group to only two items from its list during the initial reporting-out period. This will minimize duplication and ensure that each group has an opportunity to give input. Record the responses on a flipchart page.

5. After each group has had an opportunity to offer two items, solicit any items they may have on their lists that have not been mentioned and add them to the master list.

DISCUSSION QUESTIONS FOR DEBRIEFING

Discuss the activity by asking the following questions:

1. How did you feel about being asked what you want to know?

2. How does this activity relate to your expectations for this orientation session?

Learning Activity 10–7: Team Logo

OBJECTIVES

The objectives of this activity are to help participants

- ♦ develop a sense of what it's like to be part of a team

- ♦ recognize that they are part of a workplace team.

MATERIALS

The materials needed for this activity are

- ♦ flipchart pages

- ♦ markers

- ♦ masking tape.

TIME

- ♦ 30 minutes

PREPARATION

Set up a table for each team of participants expected to attend.

INSTRUCTIONS

1. Create teams of five to seven people. Direct the teams to tables around the room (or to work areas).

2. Distribute one or two sheets of flipchart paper and markers to each group.

3. Explain that the purpose of the activity is to create a logo for their team. The logo will represent their team's values, vision, or anything that distinguishes them as a newly formed team. Give them 20 minutes to create a design.

4. At the end of the time period, ask a representative from each team to post its logo on the wall.

5. Ask a representative from each team to briefly explain its logo to the rest of the participants.

VARIATION

Instead of a logo, ask each team to come up with a song title or slogan that describes it.

DISCUSSION QUESTIONS FOR DEBRIEFING

Discuss the activity by asking the following questions:

1. What was it like working as a team to create this logo?

2. What did it take to be successful in completing the task?

3. Of what value was the activity?

4. How can the experience of creating a team logo help you as a member of a new team?

Learning Activity 10–8: Orientation Bingo!

OBJECTIVES

The objectives of this activity are to help participants

- integrate into their thoughts and behavior the key words, philosophy, and concepts germane to the organization

- become familiar with organizational and industry terminology.

MATERIALS

The materials needed for this activity are

- Tool 10–2: Orientation Bingo! Sample Game Sheet

- Tool 10–3: Orientation Bingo! Sample Key Words and Concepts

- Handout 10–3: Orientation Bingo! Blank Game Sheet

- marking pen for each participant

- your choice of prizes.

TIME

- Ongoing throughout the orientation program

- 15 minutes to debrief during the orientation's closing activities

PREPARATION

1. Using copies of the blank version of the game sheet in Handout 10–3, prepare Bingo-like game sheets that contain key words and phrases specific to your organization and industry, each one in a separate box. Create a different sheet for every participant by altering the terms and their positions on the sheets.

2. Using Tool 10–3 as an example, create a handout listing organization-specific key words, concepts, philosophy, vision, mission, values, and so forth. Make one copy for each participant.

INSTRUCTIONS

1. Distribute blank game sheets and handouts to participants.

2. Explain that there are certain words or phrases associated with this organization and its culture. As team members, participants will be expected to become familiar with these terms and to make them a part of their lives at work.

3. Explain that to help them integrate these terms into their thoughts and behavior, they will have an opportunity to compete for prizes throughout the day via this Bingo-like game.

4. Explain that throughout the session, anytime they hear anyone mention a word or phrase that appears on their game sheet, they can mark it off by putting an "X" through it. When they have marked off all of the spaces in a row (vertical, horizontal, or diagonal), they can yell "Bingo!" Tell them that a prize will be awarded whenever a win occurs.

5. Throughout the day, award prizes as people complete their game sheets.

6. Before the orientation's closing activities, announce that the ongoing game is over and debrief the experience with the discussion questions below.

VARIATIONS

1. You may choose to have people compete individually or in teams.

2. You can create your game sheets with 9, 16, or 25 squares. Remember that you will need more terms than you have squares on your game sheet in order to vary the contents of the sheets.

3. You may choose to limit the number of prizes you award. If so, require participants to mark off all the boxes on the game sheet in order to win a prize.

 ## *DISCUSSION QUESTIONS FOR DEBRIEFING*

Discuss the activity by asking the following questions:

1. What did you experience through this activity?

2. What did you like or dislike about the activity?

3. How helpful was this activity in helping you learn our key terms and concepts?

4. Why is it important to learn these terms and concepts?

5. How can this knowledge help you as a new member of our team?

Tool 10–2
Orientation Bingo! Sample Game Sheet

LEAD	Safety First	Employer of Choice
Sense of Community	Serve Each Other	PRIDE
Invest in Your Future	Team Focused	WOW the Customer

Tool 10–3
Orientation Bingo! Sample Key Words and Concepts

The following are key words and phrases associated with our organization and its culture. We want you to become familiar with these terms and make them a part of your daily life here at [company name].

Employer of Choice	=	How we want to be viewed in the marketplace
Invest in Your Future	=	The organization's pension plan
LEAD	=	Our management development program
PRIDE	=	The name of our quality program
Safety First	=	A core value of this organization
Sense of Community	=	A core value of this organization
Serve Each Other	=	Our philosophy of internal service
Team Focused	=	A core value of this organization
WOW the Customer	=	Our customer service reward program

Handout 10–3

Orientation Bingo! Blank Game Sheet

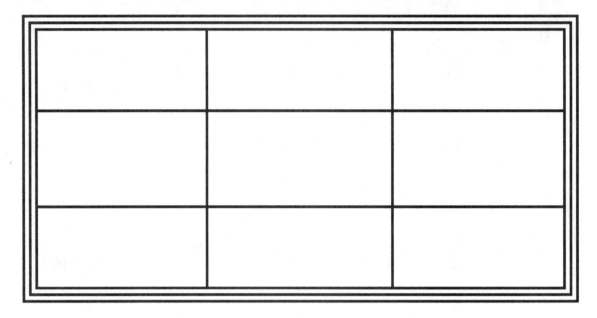

Learning Activity 10–9: What Do You Know About Our Organization?

OBJECTIVE

The objective of this activity is to help participants become familiar with the organization.

MATERIALS

The materials needed for this activity are Handout 10–4: What Do You Know? Worksheet or PowerPoint slides or transparencies 7–7 through 7–16.

TIME

◆ 15 minutes

PREPARATION

Prepare one handout for each participant or set up equipment to show slides or transparencies. You may wish to alter the questions to suit your organization.

INSTRUCTIONS

1. Tell participants that they will have an opportunity to get to know more about the organization through this next activity. Also tell them that it is a great way to showcase what they already know (or think they know) about their new employer.

2. Distribute the handout and ask them to work with a partner to fill in the blanks.

3. Reconvene the group and review their responses.

DISCUSSION QUESTIONS FOR DEBRIEFING

Discuss the activity by asking the following questions:

1. How many items were you able to answer correctly?

2. What misconceptions did you have about our organization?

3. What new information did you pick up?

4. What insights did you gain?

5. How do you feel about being a part of this organization?

Handout 10–4
What Do You Know? Worksheet

1. Our organization has _____ locations in _____ states and _____ countries.

2. We employ approximately _____ employees worldwide.

3. We have been in business _____ years.

4. Our corporate colors are _____ .

5. The CEO of our organization is _____ .

6. Our company Website is _____ .

7. The name of our company's newsletter is _____ .

8. Our best-known (or best-selling) product (or service) is _____ .

9. Our parent company is _____ .

10. Our biggest competitor is _____ .

Learning Activity 10–10: Our Heritage

OBJECTIVES

The objectives of this activity are to help participants

- learn about the company's history, key people, products and services, contribution to the community, and so forth

- become familiar with the organization's vision and mission.

MATERIALS

The materials needed for this activity are

- a video that introduces your organization to people unfamiliar with it

- flipchart pages

- pen or pencil for each participant

- markers for each group

- masking tape

- Handout 10–5: Our Heritage Worksheet.

TIME

- 30–45 minutes, depending on length of the video provided

PREPARATION

1. Preview the video so that you are thoroughly familiar with it.

2. Prepare one worksheet for each participant. You may need to alter the questions to suit the specific information provided by the video.

INSTRUCTIONS

1. Explain to the participants that they will have an opportunity to learn more about the organization by watching a video produced especially for new employees.

2. Tell them that they will be seeking particular information as they watch the video.

3. Distribute the handout and divide the group into teams of four or five. Assign each group one, two, or three questions from the handout, depending on the number of teams you have.

4. Tell participants to take notes during the video because they will be asked to pool their information at its end.

5. Show the video.

6. When the video ends, ask the members of each group to share with the other groups the key points or information they learned watching the video.

7. Distribute blank flipchart pages and markers to each group and ask them to create one master list for their group, identifying the most important pieces of information gleaned from the experience. Also instruct them to choose an official spokesperson for each group. Give them five to seven minutes to do this.

8. At the end of the designated period, ask the teams to post their lists of key points on the wall.

9. Ask each group spokesperson to clarify and give examples of the key points listed.

VARIATION

If no video is available, you might have an executive who is a good speaker present a 10-minute lecture. Participants would be assigned certain information to listen for in the lecture.

DISCUSSION QUESTIONS FOR DEBRIEFING

Discuss the activity by asking the following questions:

1. How did you feel as you watched the video?

2. How do you feel about working for this organization?

3. What insights did you gain about our organization?

4. How will these insights or learnings help you in your job?

Handout 10–5
Our Heritage Worksheet

1. What is our organization's primary philosophy?

2. How did our organization get started?

3. What is of greatest importance to our organization?

4. What is our mission?

5. What is our vision?

6. What are we most proud of?

7. What are our best-known products or services?

Learning Activity 10–11: Organizational Structure Card Sort

OBJECTIVE

The objective of this activity is to help participants become familiar with the structure of the organization.

MATERIALS

The materials needed for this activity are

- an organization chart (see sample in Tool 10–4)

- cards for sorting (see samples in Tool 10–5).

TIME

- 20 minutes

PREPARATION

1. Prior to the workshop, use Tool 10–5 as a template for preparing the cards by listing the names of your organization's divisions and the departments situated within those divisions. Photocopy the pages on heavy card stock and cut them apart.

2. Create one set of cards for every four or five people.

3. Shuffle each set of cards several times.

4. Make copies of the organization chart (one for each participant).

INSTRUCTIONS

1. Divide the participants into groups of four or five.

2. Explain to participants that you are going to help them gain a better understanding of the company's organizational structure through an activity called a Card Sort.

3. Distribute the cards. Explain that each group is receiving a stack of division cards and department cards. The division cards correspond to the categories (or divisions) of your organization. The department

cards correspond to the various departments that operate within each of those divisions.

4. Instruct each group to sort the department cards into the appropriate divisions. Inform them of how many major divisions there are and how many departments are in each division. Give groups 10 minutes to sort the cards.

5. At the end of 10 minutes, distribute copies of the organization chart, showing the divisions and their respective departments. Ask each group to check its stacks of cards against the chart and identify how well it sorted the cards.

6. Ask each group to report its results. Conduct a brief discussion and explain or clarify as necessary.

VARIATIONS

1. You may opt to use the sample organization chart and cards included in this workbook (Tools 10–4 and 10–5) in place of a chart and cards that accurately represent your organization.

2. You may choose to include the names of division heads, managers, and so forth.

DISCUSSION QUESTIONS FOR DEBRIEFING

Discuss the activity by asking the following questions:

1. How difficult was it to determine the major area where each department reports?

2. What did you learn about the organization from this activity?

3. How can this information help you in your job?

Tool 10–4

Sample Organization Chart

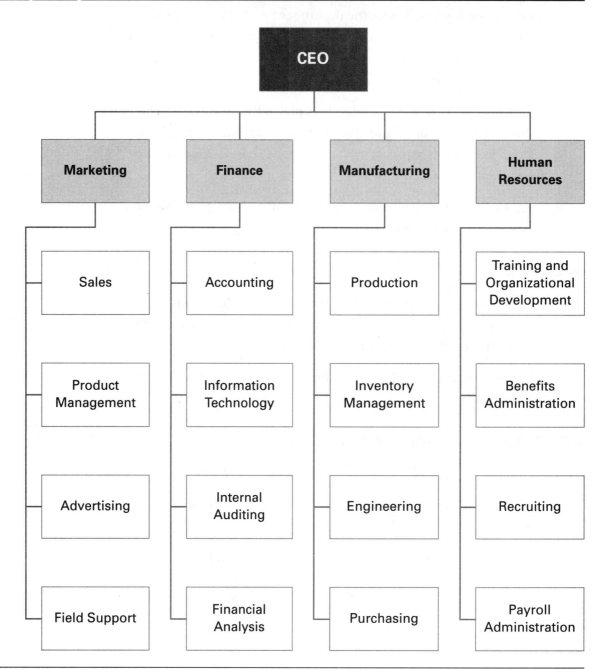

Tool 10–5

Sample Cards

Marketing	**Finance**
Manufacturing	**Human Resources**
Sales	**Accounting**

continued on next page

Tool 10–5, continued

Sample Cards

Production	**Training and Organizational Development**
Product Management	**Information Technology**
Inventory Management	**Benefits Administration**

continued on next page

Tool 10–5, continued

Sample Cards

Advertising	**Internal Auditing**
Engineering	**Recruiting**
Field Support	**Financial Analysis**

continued on next page

Tool 10–5, continued

Sample Cards

<table>
<tr>
<td>

Purchasing

</td>
<td>

Payroll Administration

</td>
</tr>
</table>

Learning Activity 10–12: Information Round Robin

OBJECTIVES

The objectives of this activity are to help participants

- ◆ gain information about key areas and departments of the organization

- ◆ meet key people from important departments in the organization

- ◆ identify how various departments contribute to the organization's goals.

MATERIALS

The materials needed for this activity will be whatever informative handouts department representatives wish to distribute.

TIME

- ◆ 60–90 minutes

PREPARATION

1. Identify and contact key people within the organization whom you want to present key pieces of information during the new employee orientation program. These people should represent major departments within the organization, such as human resources, marketing, production, accounting, and so forth.

2. Explain to guest representatives that they will be conducting round-table discussions on their areas of expertise, repeating the discussion in a series of rounds with a different group of participants each round.

3. Tell the guest speakers that they are to deliver five minutes of prepared remarks to four different groups. Their introductory remarks are meant only to provide an overview of their departments. Suggest that they have a handout to accompany their remarks. Explain that after their initial remarks, they will solicit questions from the groups of participants. Remind them that they will conduct these discussions four times with four separate groups.

4. In addition to speaking face-to-face or via telephone with these guest speakers, it is a good idea to send them the guidelines in writing.

5. Prior to the session, arrange a table and/or chairs in each of four different areas in the room where the groups can meet. Be sure that these designated discussion areas are far enough apart to ensure that groups do not disturb one another.

6. Decide how you will divide the participants into groups.

7. Decide how long each round will last, depending on the time available for the session and the number of participants. In general, 10 or 15 minutes for each round is appropriate.

INSTRUCTIONS

1. At the beginning of this activity, seat each speaker at a table or in a circle of chairs.

2. Explain to participants that they will have an opportunity to learn about the organization's various departments by interacting with representatives of various departments in an informal and personal environment.

3. Introduce each guest speaker, indicating his or her location in the room and providing a very brief background, such as the guest's position or title, responsibilities, physical location in the organization, and how long this person has been employed in the organization.

4. Create the groups and explain that these groups will remain intact and will move from area to area for each round.

5. Explain the process and time limit to the participants. Keep track of time for each round and move the groups to the next expert's area as the rounds progress.

DISCUSSION QUESTIONS FOR DEBRIEFING

Discuss the activity by asking the following questions:

1. What did you experience in this activity?

2. What did you learn?

3. How can this information help you as you begin your career here?

Learning Activity 10–13: Press Conference

OBJECTIVES

The objectives of this activity are to help participants

- ◆ learn about key areas of the organization

- ◆ meet key people from various departments or areas of the organization.

MATERIALS

The only materials needed for this activity are cards on which are written questions for audience "plants" at the press conference.

TIME

- ◆ 45–60 minutes

PREPARATION

1. Prior to the session, select four or five of the organization's key people who will present to the group vital pieces of information that are specific to their areas of responsibility in the organization.

2. Contact the presenters and explain that they will form a panel and each will deliver five to seven minutes of opening remarks, just as in an actual press conference. Remind them that they are expected to stay within their time limit and that you will have someone hold up a sign indicating when they have two minutes remaining.

3. Ask presenters to prepare questions they would like members in the audience to ask them to elicit their key pieces of information. If the presenters are reluctant to write their own questions, find out what each is going to talk about and prepare the questions yourself.

4. Ask people to be audience "plants." Give the volunteers the prepared questions and explain that they should be ready to ask the questions at the conclusion of the prepared remarks.

5. Prepare a two-minute warning sign and ask someone to act as timer.

INSTRUCTIONS

1. Introduce the activity by explaining that the participants will have an opportunity to find out more about the organization from several key people through a type of press conference.

2. Introduce the key people and briefly explain each person's position, the reason the person has been asked to speak, and what he or she will discuss.

3. Explain that each panel member will deliver five to seven minutes of opening remarks just as in an actual press conference.

4. Tell participants that after all presenters have made their opening remarks, they will then take questions from the audience. Suggest to the participants that they jot down questions as they listen to the presenters.

5. Begin the press conference by calling on the first speaker and continue until all have presented their remarks.

6. Be sure to keep the speakers on time. Be ready to interrupt, if necessary, and move on to the next presenter.

7. After the last presentation, turn to the audience and invite questions. Continue the question-and-answer period until all critical pieces of information have been addressed or until your designated time for the activity has elapsed.

VARIATION

You may want to eliminate the planted questions and simply rely on participants coming up with questions of their own.

DISCUSSION QUESTIONS FOR DEBRIEFING

Discuss the activity by asking the following questions:

1. What was your reaction to the press conference?

2. What is the most important thing you learned?

3. How can this information help you as a new employee?

Learning Activity 10–14: Poster Sessions

OBJECTIVE

The objective of this activity is to help participants identify the company's various products and services.

MATERIALS

Materials for this activity are

- ◆ product or service displays and their accompanying handouts that the marketing department or individual presenters will prepare for their poster sessions

- ◆ masking tape, easels, or other display equipment.

TIME

- ◆ 50 minutes

PREPARATION

1. Identify key products and services of the organization. Select people who are knowledgeable about those products and services to act as product and service specialists for this activity.

2. Ask each person to prepare a visual display (dimensions 3 feet by 5 feet) of the product or service he or she will represent. The poster display should be self-explanatory, that is, observers easily should understand the idea without any further written or oral explanation. (Because the posters will be displayed around the room before the program begins, participants will have an opportunity to view the posters prior to the start of the program and during breaks.) The poster should be created around materials that briefly inform, capture the imagination, and/or invite an exchange of ideas with participants.

3. Ask presenters to prepare for participants a handout that offers more detail and serves as additional reference material.

4. Ask each product/service specialist to prepare a five-minute talk describing his or her assigned product or service.

5. Each product/service specialist will remain at his or her poster for the entire activity to answer questions from participants.

INSTRUCTIONS

1. Explain to participants that they will have an opportunity to learn about various products and services through an activity called "Poster Sessions."

2. Call their attention to the posters around the room.

3. Explain that the activity will consist of four rounds. During the designated time period, department representatives will conduct five-minute presentations of their assigned product or service. Presenters also will distribute handouts.

4. Tell participants that they will have an opportunity to visit four product or service poster locations. (You may assign participants to specific locations or allow them to self-select.)

5. When you are ready to begin, tell participants that they are to move quickly to the first poster, where the specialist will explain his or her group product or service.

6. Call time at the end of each five-minute round and instruct people to move to their next poster location.

7. At the end of the fourth round, reconvene the entire group and conduct the debriefing.

8. At the end of the debriefing, encourage participants to continue their visits to the posters and talk to the specialists at the conclusion of the program.

VARIATIONS

1. Instead of using the organization's products and services, you may choose to introduce participants to the various divisions or departments within the organization. In that case, you would need to contact the departments or areas and ask them to provide displays and department representatives.

2. Instead of poster sessions to introduce the participants to the organization's products and services, you may use an activity called "Peer Lessons":

    ◆ Divide the group into smaller groups and assign each group one or two products or services.

- ◆ Distribute specific product or service descriptions to the groups responsible for that product or service.

- ◆ Give the groups 15 to 20 minutes to read about the product or service assigned and to decide how they are going to explain or demonstrate it to the rest of the group.

- ◆ At the end of the designated preparation phase, ask each group to explain its assigned product or service and solicit questions from fellow participants.

DISCUSSION QUESTIONS FOR DEBRIEFING

Discuss the activity by asking the following questions:

1. What was your reaction to the activity?

2. What did you like or dislike about the poster sessions?

3. What did you learn?

4. How can this information help you in your job?

Learning Activity 10–15:
Employees' Perspectives (Panel Discussion)

OBJECTIVES

The objectives of this activity are to help participants

- ◆ gain valuable insight into what it is really like to work for this organization

- ◆ learn about the organization from different perspectives.

TIME

- ◆ 30 minutes

PREPARATION

1. Ask three or four people who have been with the organization less than two years to participate in a panel discussion about what it's like being a new employee.

2. Ask them to think about and be ready to address specific questions, such as

   - ◆ What do you wish you would have been told during your first few weeks as a new employee?

   - ◆ What did you learn the hard way?

   - ◆ What do you like best about being employed here?

INSTRUCTION

1. Introduce the activity by explaining that participants will have an opportunity to get the "real story" of what it's like to work for this company from employees who have been with the organization less than two years.

2. Explain that the activity will be conducted as a panel discussion based on three questions. (Tell them what the questions are.)

3. Tell participants that they will have an opportunity to ask their own questions of the panelists at the end of the discussion.

4. Begin the panel discussion by asking the first question and giving each panelist an opportunity to respond. Continue this approach with the remaining questions.

5. After all panelists have addressed all the questions, solicit questions from the audience and field the questions to the appropriate panel members.

VARIATION

Instead of a panel discussion, interview two or three people in a talk-show format (called "On the Air"). After your prepared questions, invite audience members to ask questions just as they would do if they were calling in to the talk-show host.

DISCUSSION QUESTIONS FOR DEBRIEFING

Conduct a discussion by asking the following questions:

1. What was your reaction to the panel members?

2. How valuable was their information and insight?

3. What is different or unique about their perspectives?

4. How can their observations and insights help you as a new employee?

Learning Activity 10–16: Organizational Scavenger Hunt

OBJECTIVES

The objectives of this activity are to help participants

- increase their familiarity with people, places, and things in the organization

- create a sense of teamwork

- become familiar with the physical layout of the building.

MATERIALS

The materials needed for this activity are

- Handout 10–6: Organizational Scavenger Hunt Search Sheet

- Tool 10–6: Sample Scavenger Hunt Memo

- map of the building

- pen or pencil for each team

- items that you want the teams to collect (for example, business cards, brochures, forms, and so forth)

- your choice of prizes (optional).

TIME

- 60–75 minutes

PREPARATION

1. Several weeks prior to the orientation session, prepare and send a memo to all of the departments that will be involved directly or indirectly in this activity. The memo should state clearly that this activity is part of the new employee orientation and that small teams of new employees will travel throughout the building gathering items and information from different departments. Take a look at Tool 10–6 as an example.

2. Check with the departments on the day before the orientation session to remind them of the activity and to make sure that any items or materials the teams are to gather are available there.

3. Photocopy a search sheet for each team.

4. Get a map of the building for each participant.

5. Buy prizes if you plan to award them.

INSTRUCTIONS

1. Introduce the activity by explaining to participants that they will have a hands-on opportunity to gather more information about the company. Tell them that they will be traveling in small teams throughout the building to collect items or information from various departments. Further explain that although the departments are aware that they will be visiting, teams are not to be bothersome or intrusive. Also instruct them to stay together as a team at all times.

2. Divide the group into smaller groups and distribute one search sheet to each team. Try to form teams with people who will be working in different areas or departments.

3. Tell the teams that they have 40 minutes to find the items and the answers to the questions. They must return at the end of the time period, even if they have not completed their hunt.

4. Solicit questions from the groups to ensure that everyone understands the process, ask them to synchronize watches, and send them on their way.

5. As each team returns, check to see that it has found all the items and answered the questions. Also write down the time each team returns.

6. At the end of the 40 minutes, call time and reconvene the entire group. Announce the winning team—the team that gathered the most items and answers within the designated time period. If appropriate, award prizes.

VARIATION

If you want to make this activity competitive, tell the participants that the *first* team to return with all the items and the correct answers will win.

DISCUSSION QUESTIONS FOR DEBRIEFING

Discuss the activity by asking the following questions:

1. What was your reaction to the activity?

2. What items or information were the most difficult to locate? Why?

3. How well did you work as a team?

4. What was the most interesting thing you learned or discovered in your travels throughout the building?

5. What did you learn from the activity?

6. How will the information you gathered help you in your new job?

Handout 10–6

Organizational Scavenger Hunt Search Sheet

Instructions: You are going to search for the following items or information. Where an item is required, collect one as a sample from the designated area. Where information is requested, write the answer on the line provided.

1. A business card from someone in the finance department (*sample*)

2. The number of "Exit" signs on the second floor _____

3. A brochure from the marketing department (*sample*)

4. The location of the systems area _____

5. A spoon from the cafeteria (*sample*)

6. The color of the receptionist's dress, blouse, or sweater _____

7. The number of plants in the executive office waiting area _____

8. Any form from the human resources department (*sample*)

9. The color of the window coverings in the customer service area _____

10. A time card from the payroll department (*sample*)

11. A statement from any safety poster _____

12. A colored marker from the training center (*sample*)

Tool 10–6
Sample Scavenger Hunt Memo

To: All Personnel

From: [New Employee Orientation Administrator]

Date:

Subject: New Employee Orientation Program on [date]

We will be conducting a new employee orientation program for workers who have recently joined our organization. During this two-day [or one-day] program, the new employees will have an opportunity to explore the organization, locate items, and find key pieces of information that will help them become more comfortable in their new environment. This activity, called an "Organizational Scavenger Hunt," will take place at [time] on [date] and will last approximately [?] minutes.

Some of the participants may approach you for requested pieces of information or sample items. Please respond to their requests with enthusiasm and courtesy. We really want to make them feel welcome.

Thank you for your cooperation and support.

Learning Activity 10–17: Policies and Procedures Information Search

OBJECTIVE

The objectives of this activity are to help participants

- ◆ increase their knowledge and understanding of the organization's policies, procedures, and rules

- ◆ use the employee handbook as a valuable source of information

- ◆ identify the various employee benefits available to them.

MATERIALS

The materials needed for this activity are

- ◆ Handout 10–7: Policies and Procedures Information Search Worksheet

- ◆ employee handbook and other related reference material

- ◆ pen or pencil for each participant.

TIME

- ◆ 30 minutes

PREPARATION

1. Assemble the employee handbook and other related materials, as appropriate. You will need one set of materials for each group of three or four members.

2. Make one copy of Handout 10–7 for each participant.

INSTRUCTIONS

1. Explain that participants will be learning more about the organization's policies and procedures by searching for information in various resource materials.

2. Divide the group into smaller groups of three or four people. Distribute a worksheet to each participant and a set of resource materials to each group.

3. Explain that they are to work in teams using the printed material to answer the questions on the worksheet. Tell them they will have 20 minutes to complete the assignment.

4. At the end of the time period, reconvene the entire group and solicit answers to the items on the worksheet. Clarify, expand on, or provide answers to unanswered questions as necessary.

VARIATIONS

1. Instead of using this activity to familiarize participants with the employee handbook, use other company information you want them to know, such as company history or products and services. Create a relevant worksheet.

2. If the information is available to employees only online, either produce hard copies for use in the session (and explain how they can access the information online) or have the room equipped with computers on which teams can search for the information. The worksheet remains the same for this variation.

 ## DISCUSSION QUESTIONS FOR DEBRIEFING

Discuss the activity by asking the following questions:

1. How difficult was it to find the information?

2. What information did you find particularly interesting or surprising?

3. What is the most important piece of information you learned?

4. How will this information help you in your new job?

5. What was the value of this activity?

Handout 10–7
Policies and Procedures Information Search Worksheet

Instructions: Using your employee handbook and other related material, work with your team to answer the following questions.

1. When are you eligible for sick days? How many sick days do you get?

2. What constitutes sexual harassment?

3. What is the policy regarding family and medical leave?

4. When and where are employees permitted to smoke?

5. What is the difference between exempt and nonexempt employees?

6. When can you post for another job in the organization?

7. What is the standard workweek?

8. How is overtime handled?

9. When do you get paid?

10. What is considered excessive absenteeism?

11. What situations would warrant automatic discharge?

12. What is the disciplinary process?

13. How many paid holidays do you get?

14. When do you qualify for group life and health benefits?

Learning Activity 10–18:
What Do I Wear? (Agree/Disagree)

OBJECTIVE

The objective of this activity is to help participants identify the attire appropriate to their new work environment.

MATERIALS

The materials needed for this activity are

- one set of cards for each participant (one "A" card and one "D" card) (use Tool 10–7 as a template for the cards)

- PowerPoint slides or transparencies 7–17 through 7–21.

TIME

- 20 minutes

PREPARATION

1. Copy Tool 10–7 onto cardstock and trim to produce a two-card set for each participant.

2. Prepare slides showing pictures of appropriate and inappropriate clothing, accessories, and so forth.

INSTRUCTIONS

1. Explain to the group that you are going to present several statements and that they are to indicate whether they agree or disagree with the statement.

2. Distribute the two-card sets. Explain that the "A" card stands for "Agree" and the "D" card stands for "Disagree."

3. As each statement or picture is displayed or stated, participants will indicate whether they agree or disagree by holding up the appropriate card.

4. For each item, ask one person who agrees and one who disagrees to explain the reason for his or her choice. Comment on their reasons and clarify the organization's policy, as appropriate.

VARIATIONS

1. Instead of showing pictures of appropriate and inappropriate clothing and accessories, develop four to six true-and-false statements related to the organization's dress code.

2. Instead of using cards to indicate their responses, ask participants to stand if they agree and remain seated if they disagree.

DISCUSSION QUESTIONS FOR DEBRIEFING

Discuss the activity by asking the following questions:

1. What was your reaction to some of the pictures or statements that illustrated inappropriate attire?

2. How was this information similar to or different from your perception of what is appropriate?

3. How do these guidelines relate to the organization's philosophy?

4. What challenges do you foresee in adhering to these guidelines?

5. How can this information help you?

Tool 10–7

Agree/Disagree Cards

# A	# D
# A	# D
# A	# D

Learning Activity 10–19: Safety First

OBJECTIVES

The objectives of this activity are to help participants

- ◆ increase their awareness of the importance of safety in the workplace

- ◆ identify their role in and responsibility for maintaining a safe working environment.

MATERIALS

The materials needed for this activity are

- ◆ various props that can be arranged to create mock safety hazards

- ◆ Handout 10–8: Safety Hazards Worksheet.

TIME

- ◆ 20–30 minutes

PREPARATION

1. Arrange an area of the room with props that create various safety hazards. For an office environment, you could choose the following hazardous situations:

   - ◆ cup of coffee next to a computer

   - ◆ wastebasket left in the open aisle

   - ◆ desk drawer left open

   - ◆ electrical extension cords stretched across a walkway

   - ◆ overloaded electrical plugs

   - ◆ space heater

   - ◆ liquid spilled on floor

   - ◆ dim lighting

   - ◆ ladder blocking a passageway

   - ◆ scissors laying on desk

- ◆ hidden fire extinguisher

- ◆ broken swivel chair

- ◆ table with wobbly legs

- ◆ several stacked boxes

- ◆ open jar of peanut butter.

2. Make one copy of Handout 10–8 for each participant.

PROCEDURE

1. Introduce the activity by explaining that employees are injured on the job every year as a result of their own carelessness or the carelessness of their co-workers. Emphasize that maintaining a safe and healthy work environment is everyone's responsibility.

2. Tell participants that they will learn about some common and seemingly innocent safety hazards through this activity.

3. Ask participants to form pairs and distribute the safety hazard worksheet to each participant. Tell them to fill out both worksheets because they will turn one of them in when it's complete.

4. Explain that mock safety hazards have been created in another area and that their team task is to identify each potential hazard and be able to explain why it is a hazard and what they should do to prevent or correct it.

5. Tell them that the activity is competitive and that they will be judged on time, accuracy, and completeness. Also tell them that as soon as their sheets are completed, one member of the pair should bring one sheet to the facilitator. Remind them that because the activity is competitive, they should be careful not to let other pairs hear their discussions. Give them 10 minutes to complete their hazard assessments.

6. At the end of the 10 minutes, call time and note those pairs who completed their worksheets.

7. Review the safety hazards by asking volunteers to take turns identifying a hazard and explaining why it is a hazard and what to do about it. Here are some sample responses:

- cup of coffee next to a computer (can spill and damage equipment; also can create electrical problems)

- wastebasket left in the open aisle (people could trip over it)

- desk drawer left open (people could run into it and hurt themselves)

- electrical extension cords stretched across a walkway (people could trip over them)

- overloaded electrical plugs (could create electrical problems; there is the potential for fire)

- space heater (is a fire hazard)

- liquid spilled on floor (people could slip and fall)

- dim lighting (people's eyes are stressed from poor lighting)

- ladder blocking a passageway (people could run into it or it could fall on someone)

- scissors laying on desk (could cut someone or be used as a weapon)

- hidden fire extinguisher (quick and easy access is needed in case of fire)

- broken swivel chair (person could fall off chair and get hurt)

- table with wobbly legs (table could fall on someone)

- several stacked boxes (boxes could fall on someone)

- open jar of peanut butter (food attracts rodents and bugs)

8. Determine winners and award prizes.

9. Emphasize that health and safety measures are governed by the Occupational Safety and Health Administration and that a company can be fined for not following regulations. Also mention that costly workers' compensation claims can be avoided if each employee adheres to health and safety guidelines.

VARIATIONS

1. Make this activity more specific by grouping people according to the areas where they will be working. For example, those who will be

working in a manufacturing environment may have a different mock environment from those who will be in an office environment.

2. Extend the discussion by asking people to think about other health and safety hazards that were not illustrated in this activity—for example, washing hands after using the bathroom, wearing safety glasses, and so forth.

DISCUSSION QUESTIONS FOR DEBRIEFING

Discuss the activity by asking the following questions:

1. What did you experience as you were looking for the safety hazards?

2. How difficult was it to identify them?

3. What surprised you about some of the hazards?

4. What did you learn about safety issues from this activity?

5. How will this information help you on the job?

Handout 10–8

Safety Hazards Worksheet

Names of Team Members _____

Instructions: With your partner, walk around the room(s), jotting down the safety hazards that you notice. When you have identified these safety problems, work with your partner to write down the reason that the situation is hazardous and what should be done to prevent or correct it.

When each of you has completed your worksheet, give one copy to the facilitator. You will be judged on a combination of time, accuracy, and completeness.

HAZARD	WHY IT'S A HAZARD	PREVENTIVE OR CORRECTIVE ACTION

Learning Activity 10–20: Living Our Core Values

OBJECTIVES

The objectives of this activity are to help participants

- ◆ identify the organization's core values

- ◆ reflect the organization's values in their own workplace behavior.

MATERIALS

The only item needed for this activity is one copy of the organization's values statement for each participant.

TIME

- ◆ 40 minutes

PROCEDURE

1. Introduce the activity by explaining that the organization subscribes to certain values; that is, fundamental guiding beliefs that drive the way the organization competes, produces, serves, and manages. Some typical corporate values are honesty, integrity, respect, trust, teamwork, quality, and professionalism.

2. Divide the group into teams of four or five people. Distribute copies of the organization's values statement.

3. Depending on the number of values and the number of teams, assign each team one or two values and ask it to come up with examples of specific behaviors that illustrate the value(s) assigned. These examples should focus on specific employee behaviors. For example:

   - ◆ Honesty—admitting when you make a mistake

   - ◆ Respect—talking to people in a polite, civilized manner

   - ◆ Teamwork—pitching in to help even when it's not in your job description

   - ◆ Professionalism—answering the telephone in a business-like manner.

4. At the end of the designated time period, reconvene the entire group and ask the teams to share their examples.

DISCUSSION QUESTIONS FOR DEBRIEFING

Discuss the activity by asking the following questions:

1. What was your reaction to the activity?

2. How difficult was it to come up with examples of specific behaviors?

3. What did you learn about corporate values that you didn't know before?

4. How will this knowledge of corporate values influence your behavior at work?

5. How will your understanding of these values benefit you as an employee?

Learning Activity 10–21:
Taking the High Road—Ethics in the Workplace

OBJECTIVES

The objectives of this activity are to help the participant

- identify the relationship between corporate values and organizational ethics

- distinguish between ethical and unethical behavior.

MATERIALS

The materials needed for this activity are

- one copy of the organization's ethics policy for each participant

- Handout 10–9: Taking the High Road Worksheet

- pen or pencil for each participant.

TIME

- 30–45 minutes

PREPARATION

Make one copy of the ethics policy and Handout 10–9 for each participant.

INSTRUCTIONS

1. Refer participants to the organization's values statement (distributed in Learning Activity 10–20). Explain that values drive ethical behavior. Values are what we *believe;* ethics are what we *do.*

2. Distribute copies of the organization's ethics policy and explain that the commitment to conduct business lawfully and ethically is fundamental to the organization's existence and its success. Furthermore, explain that the organization expects that all employees meet the highest standards of legal and ethical behavior.

3. Point out the major ethical categories or topics, explaining briefly what each means. Typical ethics policies address the following areas:

♦ relationship with customers, suppliers, and consultants

♦ gifts or entertainment

♦ conflicts of interest

♦ proprietary information

♦ confidentiality

♦ use of company resources

♦ product integrity

♦ political activity

♦ recording and use of funds

♦ insider trading.

4. Ask participants to work in pairs to identify the value(s) that relates to each ethics category.

5. At the end of 10 minutes, reconvene the group and review their answers.

6. Next explain that it is important to understand clearly what is acceptable and unacceptable behavior. Further explain that they will have an opportunity to gain more insight into the difference between ethical and unethical behavior through a group activity.

7. Divide the group into teams of four or five people. Distribute a copy of Handout 10–9 to each team member.

8. Tell teams that they are to determine if each scenario on the worksheet is ethical or unethical and to which section or area of the ethics policy it relates. Tell them they have 15 minutes to complete the task.

9. At the end of the designated time period, reconvene the entire group and review the scenarios and teams' ethical judgments.

DISCUSSION QUESTIONS FOR DEBRIEFING

Discuss the activity by asking the following questions:

1. What was your reaction to the scenarios?

2. What did you think about or take into consideration as you were discussing the scenarios?

3. What insights did you gain about business ethics?

4. What was different from or similar to your own ideas about what is unethical behavior?

5. How will this information help you in your daily behavior at work?

Handout 10–9

Taking the High Road Worksheet

Instructions: For each of the following scenarios, identify the behavior as ethical or unethical by placing an "E" or a "U" in the second column. Then indicate to which section of the organization's ethics policy the scenario relates.

SCENARIO	E/U	SECTION OF ETHICS POLICY
1. Making personal long-distance telephone calls		
2. Taking pens, paper, and paper clips home for your teenager		
3. Sending an email to your friend to confirm your weekend party plans		
4. Working at night and on weekends for one of the company's competitors		
5. Sharing with friends some personal information about one of your customers		
6. Coming in to work 30 minutes late and not noting it on your time card		
7. Taking your spouse and your client to dinner and charging it all to your expense account		
8. Accepting a set of golf clubs from a vendor		
9. Telling friends and family members about a potential merger between your company and a competitor that you overheard two managers discussing		
10. Promising to deliver a product to a customer by a certain date, even though you know the deadline cannot be met		

Learning Activity 10–22: Whom Do I Contact?

OBJECTIVES

The objectives of this activity are to help participants

- identify whom to contact or where to go when they have questions or need information

- recognize the importance of using their own initiative and accessing the appropriate resources for information.

MATERIALS

The materials needed for this activity are

- Handout 10–10: Whom Do I Contact? Worksheet

- pen or pencil for each participant.

TIME

- 20–30 minutes

PREPARATION

Prepare a worksheet listing various questions that participants might have in their first few weeks and months on the job. Use Handout 10–10 as is or customize it. Also list various sources of information in random order. Make one copy of the worksheet for each participant.

INSTRUCTIONS

1. Distribute worksheets and tell participants that in their first few weeks and months on the job they will have questions or need information and often may be confused about where to go for help.

2. Explain that this activity is designed to help them identify the appropriate resource for the information they need. In some cases, the resource may be a person (such as their manager); in other cases, the resource may be the employee handbook or company intranet.

3. Tell participants to work with a partner and identify the appropriate resource for the information needed. Mention that each resource *can*

be used more than once. Give them 10 minutes to complete the worksheet.

4. At the end of 10 minutes, reconvene the entire group and review their responses. Clarify and explain, as necessary.

DISCUSSION QUESTIONS FOR DEBRIEFING

Discuss the activity by asking the following questions:

1. How difficult was it to match the information with the resource?

2. How helpful do you think this information will be to you in your job?

Handout 10–10
Whom Do I Contact? Worksheet

Instructions: For each topic listed below, identify the source(s) you would go to for information or help.

Organization Resources and Sources of Information:

- Immediate supervisor
- Benefits administrator
- Human resources department
- Payroll department
- Employee handbook

IF YOU WANTED TO FIND OUT ABOUT...	YOU WOULD GO TO...
1. Tuition reimbursement	
2. Time off without pay	
3. Medical coverage	
4. Problem with a co-worker	
5. Leaving work early	
6. Vacation schedule	
7. Getting a raise	
8. Payroll problems	
9. Sick days	
10. Overtime	
11. Dress code	
12. Taking breaks	

Learning Activity 10–23:
Terminology Tournament

OBJECTIVE

The objective of this activity is to help participants learn company and industry jargon and terminology.

MATERIALS

The materials needed for this activity are

- Handout 10–11: Terminology Tournament Study Sheet

- flipchart pages and markers

- pen or pencil for each participant

- mini quiz for each round (your design)

- your choice of prizes.

TIME

- 45–60 minutes

PREPARATION

1. Customize Handout 10–11 as needed and make one copy of it for each participant.

2. Prepare flipchart pages to record team scores.

3. Create three or more mini quizzes (one for each round).

INSTRUCTIONS

1. Explain that the purpose of this activity is to help participants become familiar with the jargon or terminology common to the organization and the industry.

2. Divide the group into teams of two to eight people.

3. Distribute the handout.

4. Explain that they are going to participate in a learning tournament. Tell them that this process is a combination of teamwork, individual accountability, and team competition.

5. Tell them that the tournament will consist of three or more rounds, each of which will follow the same procedure:

   ◆ People will work with a partner or "study buddy" to study the information on the handout and will take turns coaching and quizzing each other. The goal is to help one another master the information. They will have 10 minutes to study the material.

   ◆ At the end of the study session, each person will receive a mini quiz designed to test the individual's mastery of the material. Each quiz will have four or five items. For example, you would list the abbreviations and the employees would write what each abbreviation means. The quiz must be completed individually.

   ◆ At the end of the time specified for answering the questions, solicit answers from the group. Each person will self-score his or her quiz.

   ◆ Team members then will combine their scores for the round, and the facilitator will post those scores on flipchart paper. (If you do not have the same number of people in every group, calculate the average score for each team.)

   ◆ Repeat the process for as many rounds as you wish.

   ◆ At the end of the last round, calculate the total scores and award prizes.

 ## *DISCUSSION QUESTIONS FOR DEBRIEFING*

Discuss the activity by asking the following questions:

1. What was your reaction to the terminology tournament?

2. How helpful was the activity in your learning the terminology?

3. What did you find difficult or challenging?

4. How will knowing this terminology help you?

Handout 10–11
Terminology Tournament Study Sheet

CC = Client company

CPI = Continuous process improvement

CPU = Central processing unit

CSR = Customer service representative

EAP = Employee assistance program

ERC = Emergency response center

ESP = Enhanced service provider

HO = Home office

IT = Information technology

LAN = Local area network

PIP = Performance improvement plan

POS = Point of sale

QOS = Quality of service

RAM = Random access memory

SDWT = Self-directed work teams

SOP = Standard operating procedures

SR = Service request

URL = Universal resource locator

Learning Activity 10–24: Summary of Learnings

OBJECTIVE

The objective of this activity is to help participants leave the session with a clear understanding of the key learning points covered during the new employee orientation.

MATERIALS

The materials needed for this activity are

- ◆ flipchart pages
- ◆ markers
- ◆ masking tape.

TIME

- ◆ 40 minutes

INSTRUCTIONS

1. Divide the group into teams of four or five members. Give each team a flipchart sheet and a marker.

2. Give them 20 minutes to develop a list of key learning points from the program.

3. At the end of 20 minutes, call time and ask the teams to post their lists on the wall.

4. Compare the lists, citing differences and similarities.

DISCUSSION QUESTIONS FOR DEBRIEFING

Discuss the activity by asking the following questions:

1. What did you notice as you looked at the lists of key points?

2. How difficult was this activity for you?

3. What was difficult about it?

4. What was the benefit of doing this activity?

Learning Activity 10–25: Full Circle

OBJECTIVES

The objectives of this activity are to help participants

- recognize and acknowledge how well the program addressed their questions and concerns

- tie together the various sections of the program by revisiting the questions generated at the beginning of the program.

MATERIALS

For this activity you will need the flipchart pages with questions generated in Learning Activity 10–6 at the beginning of the program.

TIME

- 15 minutes

INSTRUCTIONS

1. Direct participants' attention to the flipchart pages with the Post-it notes (or group lists) that they attached to them at the beginning of the program.

2. If Post-it notes were used, ask participants to move to those pages and remove the notes they wrote if the question(s) they wrote on them were addressed in the orientation program. If you, as facilitator, have done your job, the flipchart pages will be emptied of all notes. If there are any left, be sure to address them.

3. If you used the group-generated lists, read aloud each item on each list and mark it off if participants tell you the item was addressed.

DISCUSSION QUESTIONS FOR DEBRIEFING

Discuss the activity by asking the following questions:

1. What was the value of taking back your own questions or expectations? (Their answers should reflect the fact that the participants have taken ownership for their own learning and orientation.)

2. What did you learn from the activity?

3. How will this activity help you?

Learning Activity 10–26: Reflections

OBJECTIVES

The objectives of this activity are to help participants

- express what they are going to take away from the orientation session

- experience a sense of camaraderie with the group.

MATERIALS

All you need for this exercise is a rubber ball.

TIME

- 15 minutes

INSTRUCTIONS

1. Ask participants to get up from their seats and form a circle.

2. Explain that you would like each person to express a final sentiment by stating what he or she liked best about their orientation experience.

3. Tell them that they will take turns tossing a ball from one person to another. The person who has possession of the ball will offer his or her thought and then toss the ball to someone else.

4. You begin the activity by expressing your personal sentiment and then tossing the ball to any one of the participants. The ball toss continues until everyone has spoken.

VARIATION

1. Instead of a rubber ball, use a ball of yarn. Toss the yarn to a participant and ask that person to state briefly what he or she has gained from the orientation experience.

2. Ask that person to hold on to the loose end of the yarn and toss the ball to another person.

3. This process continues until each person is holding a segment of the yarn and has expressed his or her sentiments. Note that every person should now be connected by the yarn.

4. Mention that although they began the orientation program as individuals from different backgrounds, they are leaving to start their new job experiences as part of something bigger than themselves.

5. Cut the yarn with scissors so that each person takes a piece of yarn as a reminder of the experience and of their fellow new employees.

Learning Activity 10–27: Group Photo and End-of-Program Questionnaire

OBJECTIVES

The objectives of this activity are to help participants

- ◆ develop a sense of community and camaraderie
- ◆ celebrate the orientation experience.

MATERIALS

For this activity you will need

- ◆ a digital camera
- ◆ Handout 10–12: End-of-Program Questionnaire.

TIME

- ◆ 15–20 minutes

PREPARATION

Make one copy of the questionnaire for each of the participants.

INSTRUCTIONS

1. Ask participants to assemble themselves for a group photo.

2. Explain that this will give each person a remembrance of their shared experience because everyone will receive a copy of the photo.

3. Take a picture of the group and express your own final sentiments.

4. Ask if anyone else would like to make any parting remarks.

5. Thank everyone for participating in the program. Distribute the end-of-program questionnaire and ask them to complete it and leave it with you as they leave the room. Wish them great success in their new jobs and send them on their way!

VARIATIONS

1. In addition to passing out the individual copies of the photo, post the picture (along with the employees' names and assigned departments)

on the organization's intranet to introduce and welcome the new workers to the rest of the organization.

2. Post the picture on a bulletin board or include it in the company newsletter.

◆ ◆ ◆

The following chapter presents useful checklists, memos, and letters that will help you develop and implement your organization- and department-level orientation programs.

Handout 10–12

End-of-Program Questionnaire

New Employee Orientation Participant Feedback

Thank you for participating in this program. Your feedback about the content, class structure, and facilitator(s) is very valuable. Please take a moment and let us know the value of this program to you as a new employee of the organization. Circle the appropriate answer for each question below, and add your comments.

1. To what degree did the facilitator(s) create an atmosphere in which you felt comfortable participating and interacting with others?

   HIGH DEGREE   MODERATE DEGREE   LOW DEGREE   NOT AT ALL

   Comments :

2. How would you rate the facilitator(s) in terms of ability to communicate the information?

   EXCELLENT   GOOD   FAIR   POOR

   Comments :

3. To what degree was/were the facilitator(s) responsive to individual questions and concerns?

   HIGH DEGREE   MODERATE DEGREE   LOW DEGREE   NOT AT ALL

   Comments :

4. How would you rate the learning materials (workbook, visual aids, handouts)?

   EXCELLENT   GOOD   FAIR   POOR

   Comments :

5. How would you rate the learning activities (get-acquainted activities, discussions, small-group activities, pairs activities)?

   EXCELLENT   GOOD   FAIR   POOR

   Comments :

continued on next page

Handout 10–12, continued
End-of-Program Questionnaire

6. To what degree will the information learned in the program help you as a new employee?

   HIGH DEGREE   MODERATE DEGREE   LOW DEGREE   NOT AT ALL

   Comments :

7. What overall rating would you give this program?

   EXCELLENT   GOOD   FAIR   POOR

   Comments:

8. What topics should we have spent *more* time discussing?

9. What topics should we have spent *less* time discussing?

10. What suggestions do you have for enhancing this program?

♦

Helpful Checklists and Other Tools

What's in This Chapter?

♦ Eleven tools for line managers, supervisors, and facilitators implementing new employee orientation programs

♦ Follow-up participant survey to assess program utility and results 90 days after the orientation

Developing, implementing, and maintaining an effective new employee orientation program is not easy, especially when there are so many others involved. Those who play a role in this process will have other responsibilities and so may give a low priority to their orientation assignment. Line managers and supervisors, in particular, are so busy with the day-to-day operation of their departments that they may be reluctant to devote the time necessary to plan and prepare for a new employee. They may need some additional tools to make it easier to fulfill their responsibilities in assimilating the new employee into the new work environment.

This chapter includes sample checklists and memos that easily are adapted to each organization's specific needs and circumstances. These job aids can help streamline the process and ensure that nothing is overlooked or forgotten. Creating and using such tools also helps ensure consistency of the new employee orientation process throughout the organization.

Tool 11–1: Sample Welcome Letter

The welcome letter is an important part of the new employee orientation process. Its primary purpose is twofold:

1. It confirms specific details about the position.

2. It assures the employee that he or she has made the right decision in joining your organization.

The welcome letter should contain the following elements:

1. an enthusiastic and genuine statement of welcome

2. details of the position:

    ◆ job title

    ◆ start date and time

    ◆ site location

    ◆ brief job description

    ◆ name of supervisor

3. forms to sign and things to read

4. review of reasons the person was chosen (relate them to skills and qualities)

5. an offer to answer questions.

Tool 11–1
Sample Welcome Letter

Dear _____:

Welcome to [name of organization]! We are so excited that you have decided to join our team as a [job title] in the [department/branch, and so forth]. Your skills and experience in [specifically mention] are just what we are looking for to enhance our operation in the [mention function] area.

We look forward to your arrival on [date and time] at our [location]. Please report to the security area and ask for [name of supervisor or human resources representative].

To help you prepare for your first day, I have enclosed the following information for your review:

- your job description
- our annual report
- descriptions of our products and services
- overview of our benefits package
- building layout.

I also have enclosed several forms to complete and return before your first day. The completed forms will enable us to process the paperwork and have all the appropriate credentials, such as your identification badge, parking permit, and security codes, ready for you when you arrive.

In the meantime, if you have any questions, you may contact me at [phone number] or your supervisor [name] at [phone number].

We're pleased you have accepted our offer, and we look forward to a long, productive, and rewarding employment relationship.

Sincerely,

Tool 11–2: Sample Memo to the New Employee's Co-workers

The supervisor plays a pivotal role in making the new employee feel welcome in the department. To that end, the supervisor should prepare the staff for the new worker's arrival. No matter how small or informal the group may be, the supervisor should send a memo to all department employees, telling them the name of the new employee, when the employee will arrive, what he or she will be doing, where he or she will be located, and such information as the new person's previous job, background, or qualifications.

Tool 11–2
Sample Memo to the New Employee's Co-workers

To: [Department] Team Members

From: [Name of Manager/Supervisor]

Date:

Subject: New Team Member

I am pleased to announce that [new employee's name] will be joining our team as a [job title/responsibility]. [Employee's name] comes to us with many years of experience in the areas of [provide some details].

[New employee's name]'s first day will be [date]. I have asked [name of co-worker] to be [new employee's name]'s buddy. Although [name of co-worker] officially will be responsible for guiding our newest team member through [his/her] first few days, I am asking that each of you make it a point to welcome [new employee's name] to our group.

Thank you for helping make [new employee's name]'s transition a smooth and pleasant experience.

Tool 11-3: Tasks to Do Before the New Employee's First Day

Because the relationship between the new employee and the supervisor is so important, the supervisor should make every effort to help the employee become comfortable in his or her new environment. The supervisor's personal involvement (including communication, preparation, and planning) is critical. This checklist suggests actions the supervisor should take even before the employee's first day on the job.

Tool 11–3
Tasks to Do Before the New Employee's First Day

Instructions: Place a checkmark in the box adjacent to each task when it is completed.

☐ Call the new employee and welcome him or her to the team.

☐ Send a memo to staff informing them of the new employee's arrival.

☐ Prepare the new employee's work area.

☐ Create a checklist of activities for the new employee's first day.

☐ Create a checklist of information to communicate to the new worker during his or her first day.

☐ Create a checklist of activities to complete during the new employee's first week on the job.

☐ Assign a staff member to serve as a mentor or buddy to the new employee.

☐ Meet with the assigned mentor to discuss your expectations of his or her interaction with the new employee.

☐ Schedule time to spend with the new worker on his or her first day and throughout the first week.

☐ _____

☐ _____

Tool 11–4: Materials to Send Before the New Employee's First Day

The more information the new worker has about the organization and what is expected, the more quickly he or she will feel comfortable in the new job. This checklist suggests materials and information that the new employee should receive when the employment agreement has been reached. If possible, these materials should accompany the welcoming letter. In most cases, the human resources department will forward the materials directly to the new worker.

Tool 11–4
Materials to Send Before the New Employee's First Day

Instructions: Place a checkmark in the box adjacent to each item that is sent.

☐ Confirmation/welcome letter

☐ Job description

☐ Starting salary and other compensation details

☐ Start date

☐ First-day reporting process (where, when, to whom)

☐ Location map and directions

☐ Organization's annual report

☐ Brochures describing the organization's products and services

☐ Copy of the employee newsletter

☐ Organizational chart

☐ Benefit plan information

☐ Parking information and sticker

☐ Supervisor's name, location, and telephone number

☐ Forms to be completed

☐ Request for any required documents (proof of citizenship, driver's license, and so forth)

☐ _____

☐ _____

Tool 11–5: New Employee's Work Area Preparation Checklist

The supervisor should make sure that the new employee's work area is ready when he or she arrives. The way in which the work area has been prepared creates a powerful first impression. Paying careful attention to details and making sure the new employee has everything he or she needs to be a full-fledged member of the team is critical to creating a positive environment.

Tool 11–5

Preparation of the New Employee's Work Area Checklist

Instructions: Place a checkmark in the box adjacent to each item provided in the work area.

☐   Desk/work area

☐   Password for access to computer system

☐   Telephone

☐   Computer

☐   Identification badge

☐   Organization telephone directory

☐   Supplies

☐   Safety equipment

☐   Uniform

☐   Keys, locker assignment, and so forth

☐   Parking sticker

☐   Job description

☐   Name plate

☐   Business cards

☐   _____

☐   _____

Tool 11–6: Activities for the New Employee's First Day

The supervisor must devote a significant amount of time to the employee that first day on the job. Although some of the items on this checklist may seem trivial, they are important in making the new employee feel welcome. The supervisor should take personal responsibility for making sure the new employee has all the materials he or she needs to feel a part of the team.

Tool 11–6
Activities for the New Employee's First Day

Instructions: Place a checkmark in the box adjacent to each activity completed.

☐ Personally greet the new employee.

☐ Introduce the new employee to co-workers.

☐ Conduct a tour of the building and work site.

☐ Assign a buddy or mentor.

☐ Provide an overview of the department and its relationship to the rest of the organization.

☐ Review job description, responsibilities, and work schedule.

☐ Have the employee complete required forms.

☐ Orient the employee to his or her desk or work station.

☐ Review organization and departmental policies and procedures (refer to the employee handbook).

☐ Accompany the employee on breaks.

☐ Take the employee to lunch.

☐ Give the employee supplies, equipment, keys, uniform, and so forth.

☐ Give the employee company identification.

☐ Give the employee a parking permit and information.

☐ Show the employee how to operate various pieces of equipment.

☐ Show the employee how to complete a time card.

☐ Provide a list of key terms used in the department and organization.

☐ Meet with the employee at day's end to answer questions, review important information, give encouragement, and reinforce how happy everyone is to have him or her on the team.

☐ _____

☐ _____

Tool 11–7: Information to Communicate During the New Employee's First Day

To begin acclimating the new employee to the actual work environment, the supervisor should conduct a tour of the work site, pointing out specific equipment and significant locations of key resources. In addition, the supervisor should instruct the new employee on how to use pieces of equipment and how to follow key procedures. This checklist identifies the critical information the new employee needs to receive on his or her first day on the job.

Tool 11–7

Information to Communicate During the New Employee's First Day

Instructions: Place a checkmark in the box adjacent to each item when it has been explained to the new worker.

☐ Complete required employment forms

☐ Identification badge

☐ Location of restroom

☐ Location of break room or rest area

☐ Location of smoking area

☐ Operation of telephone

☐ How to send and receive email

☐ Location and operation of copier

☐ Location and operation of fax machine

☐ Location and operation of fire extinguishers

☐ First aid station

☐ Emergency exits and procedures

☐ Mail room location

☐ Mail procedures

☐ Time clock

☐ Worker's hours

☐ File locations, file retrieval procedures, filing scheme, and so forth

☐ Supply room

☐ Storage locations

☐ Employee lunch room or cafeteria

☐ Lockers

☐ Conference rooms

☐ _____

☐ _____

Tool 11–8: Suggested First-Day Work-Related Assignments

Although the first day generally will be devoted to getting acclimated to the new environment, it is important that the new team member begin to get a sense of what the job and the work unit are all about. This checklist suggests activities that the new employee can do with little or no direct supervision.

Tool 11–8
Suggested First-Day Work-Related Assignments

Instructions: Place a checkmark in the box adjacent to the tasks assigned and completed on the employee's first day.

☐　Review files and projects from predecessor.

☐　Review organization and product information.

☐　Practice using various equipment.

☐　Set up work area with supplies, filing system, and so forth.

☐　Set up meetings with key people—those with whom the new employee must interact regularly.

☐　Review procedures manuals.

☐　Work on a process, procedure, or task related to the job.

☐　Observe a co-worker operating in a similar position or with similar responsibilities.

☐　Complete necessary forms and paperwork.

☐　Accurately complete a time card.

☐　Answer the telephone according to department or organization standards.

☐　Log onto the email/intranet system.

☐　_____

☐　_____

Tool 11–9: Activities for the New Employee's First Week

The entire first week sets the tone for the employee's relationship with the supervisor and with the rest of the staff. The focus of the first week should be on helping the worker understand the big picture and how he or she fits into it. This checklist identifies topics for discussion between the supervisor and the new employee.

Tool 11–9
Activities for the New Employee's First Week

Instructions: Place a checkmark in the box adjacent to the activities assigned and completed by the new worker.

☐   Review department goals and priorities.

☐   Explain the relationship of the employee's job to others in the department.

☐   Discuss performance standards and expectations.

☐   Explain the performance evaluation process.

☐   Review overtime requirements.

☐   Discuss department policies and procedures.

☐   Explain career development options.

☐   Begin structured on-the-job training.

☐   _____

☐   _____

☐   _____

☐   _____

☐   _____

☐   _____

Tool 11–10: Sample Memo to New Employees

It is the job of the new employee orientation program administrator to set the tone well ahead of the actual formal orientation session. The first steps are to contact the new employee with an invitation to the formal program and to explain the benefits he or she will realize from the experience.

Tool 11–10
Sample Memo to New Employees

To: [New Employee's Name]

From: [Name], Program Facilitator

Date:

Subject: New Employee Orientation, [Date]

I invite you to attend a New Employee Orientation Program to be held [in/at location] on [date(s)] from [starting time] to [closing time].

We know that learning a new job and adjusting to a totally new organization can be challenging and sometimes overwhelming. With that in mind, we developed this program to help you and your fellow new team members feel more comfortable in your new environment.

The program has been designed to be enlightening, enriching, and entertaining. During this fast-paced, high-energy session, you will have several opportunities to

- become more knowledgeable about our organization and its rich history
- meet new colleagues and team members
- be introduced to key people within our organization
- learn about the policies and procedures that determine how we operate
- identify where to go for information or answers to questions
- become more familiar with organization and industry terminology
- gain information about key areas of the organization
- identify the tangible and intangible benefits of working here
- develop a sense of being a part of the team
- have fun!

Please confirm your attendance by [state who to contact, how, and by what date]. We look forward to seeing you!

Tool 11–11: Sample Memo to Guest Presenters and Facilitators

The success of the organization-wide new employee orientation program depends on the involvement of many people within the organization. Remember that this assignment is only a small part of the guest facilitator's responsibilities. Also keep in mind that those who have agreed to participate in the program may not be comfortable in the role of facilitator.

The program administrator needs to help prepare the guest facilitators by coaching them for their portion of the program. First, invite them to a briefing session prior to the scheduled date.

Tool 11–11
Sample Memo to Guest Presenters and Facilitators

To: [Name of Presenter or Facilitator]

From: [Name], Program Administrator

Date:

Subject: New Employee Orientation Session, [Date]

Once again, thank you for agreeing to participate in our New Employee Orientation Program. Your contribution is what has made this program such a success.

To help you prepare for your segment of the program, I have included a complete facilitator's information kit with the following items:

- ◆ memo to participants
- ◆ detailed agenda and timelines
- ◆ facilitator guidelines
- ◆ list of new employees attending the session.

Please attend a facilitators' briefing session on [date, a week before session] in [meeting location] at [time]. We will review the program design and answer any questions or concerns you may have about your role and responsibilities in this exciting program.

Tool 11–12: 90-Day Follow-up Survey

A follow-up survey is essential if you really want to know the value of your new employee orientation program. Survey new employees approximately 90 days after they started with the organization. After being on the job three months, they have settled into a routine and are more comfortable with the organization and their team members. The new employees are then in a much better position to reflect on what they learned in the orientation program and how that information has helped them adjust to their new environment.

Tool 11–12

90-Day Follow-up Survey

Instructions: To determine the true success of the new employee orientation program in meeting your needs, we are asking you to complete this follow-up survey. Your answers will help us assess the effectiveness of the program and identify ways in which we can make it more beneficial to those who attend in the future. We value your feedback and encourage you to be honest and frank.

1. Please put a checkmark in the appropriate box to evaluate the following areas covered in the orientation program in terms of their usefulness to you as a new employee of this organization. To refresh your memory of the specific program content, please refer to your participant workbook.

TOPIC	OF LITTLE HELP	SOMEWHAT HELPFUL	DEFINITELY HELPFUL	OF GREAT HELP
___ Organization history/culture	☐	☐	☐	☐
___ Organization mission, vision, values, goals	☐	☐	☐	☐
___ Organization structure	☐	☐	☐	☐
___ Compensation and benefits	☐	☐	☐	☐
___ Policies and procedures	☐	☐	☐	☐
___ Employee programs, services, resources	☐	☐	☐	☐
___ Terminology	☐	☐	☐	☐
___ Products and services	☐	☐	☐	☐

Now, on the lines to the left of the topics above, put an "M" next to the topic you found most helpful and an "L" next to the topic you found least helpful.

2. How has the information you acquired in the program helped you adjust to your new job and new environment? Be specific.

3. What were the *two* most important benefits that you received from the program?

4. What do you still want or need to know more about?

Additional comments:

◆

Using the Compact Disc

Insert the CD and locate the file *How to Use This CD.txt*.

Contents of the CD

The compact disc that accompanies this workbook on new employee orientation contains three types of files. All of the files can be used on a variety of computer platforms.

- ◆ **Adobe .pdf documents.** These include handouts and training tools.

- ◆ **Microsoft PowerPoint presentation.** The presentation adds interest and depth to several training activities included in the workbook.

- ◆ **Microsoft PowerPoint file of overhead transparency masters.** This file makes it easy to print viewgraphs in black-and-white rather than using an office copier. They contain text only; there are no images to print in greyscale.

Computer Requirements

To read or print the .pdf files on the CD, you must have Adobe Acrobat Reader software installed on your system. The program can be downloaded free of cost from the Adobe Website, *www.adobe.com*.

To use or adapt the contents of the PowerPoint presentation files on the CD, you must have Microsoft PowerPoint software installed on your system. If you simply want to view the PowerPoint documents, you must have an appropriate viewer installed on your system. Microsoft provides various viewers free for downloading from its Website, *www.microsoft.com.*

Printing from the CD

TEXT FILES

You can print the assessments and handouts using Adobe Acrobat Reader. Simply open the .pdf file and print as many copies as you need. The following documents can be directly printed from the CD:

- Handout 10–1: Connections Worksheet

- Tool 10–1: Famous Fictional Friends and Families

- Handout 10–2: At the Movies Participant Instructions

- Tool 10–2: Orientation Bingo! Sample Game Sheet

- Tool 10–3: Orientation Bingo! Sample Key Words and Concepts

- Handout 10–3: Orientation Bingo! Blank Game Sheet

- Handout 10–4: What Do You Know? Worksheet

- Handout 10–5: Our Heritage Worksheet

- Tool 10–4: Sample Organization Chart

- Tool 10–5: Sample Cards

- Handout 10–6: Organizational Scavenger Hunt Search Sheet

- Tool 10–6: Sample Scavenger Hunt Memo

- Handout 10–7: Policies and Procedures Information Search Worksheet

- Tool 10–7: Agree/Disagree Cards

- Handout 10–8: Safety Hazards Worksheet

- Handout 10–9: Taking the High Road Worksheet

- Handout 10–10: Whom Do I Contact? Worksheet

- Handout 10–11: Terminology Tournament Study Sheet

- Handout 10–12: End-of-Program Questionnaire

- Tool 11–1: Sample Welcome Letter

- Tool 11–2: Sample Memo to the New Employee's Co-workers

- Tool 11–3: Tasks to Do Before the New Employee's First Day

- Tool 11–4: Materials to Send Before the New Employee's First Day

- Tool 11–5: New Employee's Work Area Preparation Checklist

- Tool 11–6: Activities for the New Employee's First Day

- Tool 11–7: Information to Communicate During the New Employee's First Day

- Tool 11–8: Suggested First-Day Work-Related Assignments

- Tool 11–9: Activities for the New Employee's First Week

- Tool 11–10: Sample Memo to New Employees

- Tool 11–11: Sample Memo to Guest Presenters and Facilitators

- Tool 11–12: 90-Day Follow-up Survey

POWERPOINT SLIDES

You can print the presentation slides directly from this CD using Microsoft PowerPoint. Simply open the .ppt files and print as many copies as you need. You can also make handouts of the presentations by printing 2, 4, or 6 "slides" per page. These slides will be in color, with design elements embedded. PowerPoint also permits you to print these in grayscale or black-and-white, although printing from the overhead masters file will yield better black-and-white representations. Many trainers who use personal computers to project their presentations bring along viewgraphs, just in case there are glitches in the system.

Adapting the PowerPoint Slides

You can modify or otherwise customize the slides by opening and editing them in the appropriate application. However, you must retain the denotation of the original source of the material—it is illegal to pass it off as your own work. You may indicate that a document was adapted from this workbook, written and copyrighted by Karen Lawson and published by ASTD. The

Table A–1
Navigating Through a PowerPoint Presentation

KEY	POWERPOINT "SHOW" ACTION
Space bar *or* Enter *or* Mouse click	Advance through custom animations embedded in the presentation
Backspace	Back up to the last projected element of the presentation
Escape	Abort the presentation
B *or* b B *or* b *(repeat)*	Blank the screen to black Resume the presentation
W *or* w W *or* w *(repeat)*	Blank the screen to white Resume the presentation

files will open as "Read Only," so before you adapt them you will need to save them onto your hard drive under a different filename.

Showing the PowerPoint Presentations

On the CD, the following PowerPoint presentation is included: *New Employees.ppt.* Having the presentation in .ppt format means that it automatically shows full-screen when you double-click on its filename. You also can open Microsoft PowerPoint and launch it from there.

Use the space bar, the enter key, or mouse clicks to advance through a show. Press the backspace key to back up. Use the escape key to abort a presentation. If you want to blank the screen to black while the group discusses a point, press the B key. Pressing it again restores the show. If you want to blank the screen to a white background, do the same with the W key. Table A–1 summarizes these instructions.

We strongly recommend that trainers practice making presentations before using them in training situations. You should be confident that you can cogently expand on the points featured in the presentations and discuss the methods for working through them. If you want to engage your training participants fully (rather than worrying about how to show the next slide), become familiar with this simple technology *before* you need to use it. A good practice is to insert notes into the *Speaker's Notes* feature of the PowerPoint program, print them out, and have them in front of you when you present the slides.

For Further Reading

Barbazette, Jean. *Successful New Employee Orientation* (2d edition). San Francisco: Jossey-Bass/Pfeiffer, 2001.

Grabmeier, Jeff. "Employee Orientation Programs Help Build Commitment, Study Finds," *Research News* (March 28, 2000), online, Internet: http://www.osu.edu/units/research/archive/oriprgrm.htm, accessed 15 August 2001.

James, W.B., and M.W. Galbraith. "Perceptual Learning Styles: Implications and Techniques for the Practitioner." *Lifelong Learning* (January 1985), pp. 20–23.

Kirkpatrick, Donald. *Evaluating Training Programs: The Four Levels*. San Francisco: Berrett-Koehler, 1994.

Knowles, Malcolm. *The Adult Learner: A Neglected Species* (4th edition). Houston: Gulf Publishing, 1990.

Lawson, Karen. *Improving On-the-Job Training and Coaching*. Alexandria, VA: American Society for Training & Development, 1997.

Lawson, Karen. *The Trainer's Handbook*. San Francisco: Jossey-Bass/Pfeiffer, 1998.

Mantyla, Karen. *Interactive Distance Learning Exercises that Really Work!* Alexandria, VA: American Society for Training & Development, 1999.

Sims, Doris M. *Creative New Employee Orientation Programs*. New York: McGraw-Hill, 2002.

◆

Karen Lawson is an international consultant, author, and executive coach. She has extensive consulting and workshop experience in the areas of management, team development, communication, and quality service across a wide range of industries, including financial services, pharmaceutical, chemical, manufacturing, health care, and government.

In her consulting work with *Fortune* 500 companies and small businesses, she uses her experience and knowledge of human interaction to help leaders at all levels make a difference in their organizations. A much sought-after speaker at regional and national professional conferences, she informs, inspires, and involves her audiences as she shares her insights on influencing others. She is one of about 300 people worldwide to have earned the Certified Speaking Professional (CSP) designation awarded by the 4,000-member National Speakers Association.

Lawson has held many key leadership positions in professional organizations, including the American Society for Training & Development and the National Speakers Association. She also has received numerous professional awards for her contributions to the training profession.

She holds a doctorate degree in adult and organizational development from Temple University. She earned her master of arts degree from the University of Akron and bachelor of arts degree from Mount Union College. She is also a graduate of the National School of Banking in Fairfield, Connecticut.

Lawson is the author of seven books: *The Art of Influencing; The Trainer's Handbook; Train-the-Trainer Facilitator's Guide; Improving Workplace Performance Through Coaching; Improving On-the-Job Training and Coaching; 50 Communications Activities;* and *Involving Your Audience: Making It Active.* She also co-authored *101 Ways to Make Training Active,* has contributed to a number of anthologies, and has written dozens of articles in professional journals.